Competition in the Investment Banking Industry

Competition in the Investment Banking Industry

Samuel L. Hayes III
A. Michael Spence
David Van Praag Marks

Harvard University Press
Cambridge, Massachusetts
and London, England   1983

Library of Congress Cataloging in Publication Data

Hayes, Samuel L.
  Competition in the investment banking industry.

  Includes index.
  1. Investment banking—United States.   2. Investment
banking—United States—Consolidation.   3. Investment
banking—United States—Mathematical models.   I. Spence,
A. Michael (Andrew Michael)   II. Marks, David Van Praag.
III. Title.
HG4930.5.H39   1983   332.1'754   82-18685
ISBN 0-674-15415-0

Acknowledgments

The original impetus for this research was provided several years ago by a request to assist the Antitrust Division of the Justice Department in analyzing the competitive implications of an impending merger of two leading securities firms. We were asked to focus our efforts on the underwriting–corporate finance sector.

Subsequently, we decided to compile profiles of the corporate clients of the leading investment banking firms to supplement the insights provided by aggregate data. As we put the various parts of the research together, it became clear that a work of book length would be required to present the complete picture.

Many individuals and organizations assisted us in this effort. The Justice Department aided our work on concentration contained in Chapter 2. Robert Hauberg, Jr., Dan Schneider, and Terrence Fancher of its staff were particularly helpful. We are also grateful for Alan Kantrow's valuable assistance in producing the historical chapter and to Vincent Carosso for his critical review of it.

We are indebted to George Rozanski for competently handling the difficult computer work underlying the logit analysis, and to a series of other student assistants who aided in various research tasks. We are also grateful for the financial support provided by the Harvard Business School through its Division of Research under the leadership of Raymond Corey.

A number of people reviewed all or part of the manuscript at various stages in its development. These include Jeffrey Schaefer, Dan Schneider, George Parker, Warren Law, Jerry Hausman, and Dennis Logue. We are also grateful to a number of investment banking firms to which earlier versions of the work were sent for review, and to Michael Aronson and Camille Smith of Harvard University Press.

Very special thanks go to Ms. Duncan Bauer—our invaluable secretary, friend, and mentor—who oversaw production of the various drafts of the book, and who tied up innumerable loose ends along the way.

Although we have benefited from the contributions of many people, we of course assume full responsibility for the final product.

Contents

Competition in the Investment Banking Industry

Introduction

In broadest terms, the securities industry consists of firms engaged in activities related to issuing, distributing, and selling securities and related financial products. Such activities include underwriting and other investment banking activities, brokerage, and market-making. Of course, various other financial institutions, including commercial banks, provide some of the same services as securities firms. Conversely, some securities firms are diversifying their activities to include services traditionally provided by other financial institutions: de facto checking accounts,[1] loans (against margin accounts), insurance, and real estate investment portfolios.

This overlap notwithstanding, it appears reasonable to consider the securities industry as a distinct line of commerce. Securities firms appear to have a significant competitive advantage in performing investment banking and brokerage-related services, and they have generally been perceived by the business community to be the primary source of such services. The Banking Act of 1933 (the Glass-Steagall Act) currently excludes banks from many securities activities. In addition, all securities firms are uniquely subject to federal and state statutes; they are regulated by a variety of federal and industry organizations, most notably the Securities and Exchange Commission (SEC).

At the end of 1981, 392 member firms of the New York Stock

Exchange (NYSE) were doing a public business. This number was noticeably smaller than the 444 NYSE firms operating at the end of 1973. The decline in the number of firms contrasts with the sharp increase in total gross revenues attributable to the registered NYSE firms each year; these revenues increased from $4.8 billion in 1973 to $19.8 billion in 1981.[2]

Wide differences of geographic scope, style, and product mix occur among the NYSE member firms. Many do some brokerage and some investment banking; at this writing only about 12 firms provide brokerage service nationwide, and approximately 20 firms operate corporate finance departments that generate and distribute sizable new issues for major corporations. Thus, it is not surprising that in 1981 the leading 25 firms took in 74.4 percent of the industry's gross revenue and held 71.5 percent of the capital funds.[3]

Historically, many of the securities firms have specialized in one or more of the product market areas, such as institutional brokerage, retail brokerage, exchange floor brokerage, or corporate and municipal finance. Other firms have engaged in a relatively full range of securities activities, but limited themselves to a particular region of the country. A few have concentrated their activities on a particular industry, such as oil and gas. In recent years many of the national, New York–based firms have made substantial efforts to broaden their lines of business, and the traditional distinctions have in many cases become blurred.

Competition within the brokerage and secondary market-making sectors of the securities business has received considerable public attention in recent years.[4] Certainly the greater part of the consolidation activity during the past decade has involved firms with activities heavily concentrated in these areas. Despite its important contribution to the securities industry's revenue stream, competition in the capital-raising and financial services sector— that is, in the classic "investment banking" business—has drawn relatively little public attention since the celebrated federal antitrust suit against Morgan Stanley and 16 other investment banks initiated in 1947. However, a number of more recent events and trends have served to raise anew questions about the quality and patterns of competition within investment banking. The merger of White Weld into Merrill Lynch in 1978 and the combination of Lehman Brothers and Kuhn Loeb shortly thereafter, for instance, raised questions about how to measure the probable impact of such consolidations on investment banking competition.

Securities firms without a substantial history of involvement in classic investment banking have long eyed this unusually profitable end of the business with envy. In recent years they have committed massive resources to gearing themselves up to compete for lucrative corporate finance business. To what extent is this changing the competitive equation in this line of commerce?

Commercial banks and other financial service organizations have been making a determined effort to edge their way into investment banking activities. This is true not only of domestic banks, but also of foreign banks with merchant banking competence developed in other markets around the world that have sought to enter the U.S. investment banking market.

The targets of these business-generating efforts have also been undergoing change, thus creating new challenges for the intermediaries who wish to service them. Important changes in money sources and investment product preferences within the capital markets have helped to foster more sophisticated in-house financial management expertise in U.S. businesses. Thus, some financing activities whose structure and timing had in the past been largely controlled by outside investment banking advisers are now being handled largely by the issuer's own treasurer's staff. In these cases, investment banks primarily provide syndication and distribution services, which are fairly homogenized, commodity-like services compared to traditional financial structuring services.

It is within this context that the research summarized in this book was pursued. To provide a perspective on the classic investment banking business as it has evolved over time, Chapter 1 reviews the origins and development of the industry, beginning with its European roots and then tracing patterns of industry structure and practice as they evolved in response to both market and regulatory changes. After this historical sketch, in Chapter 2 we examine contemporary competition in investment banking during a period in the 1970s that was characterized by substantial change both within the securities industry and in the external economic environment. This examination focuses on trends in the concentration of public financing business of corporate clients, specifically the large and relatively self-contained market for corporate negotiated public underwritings. Many strategists in investment banking value a prominent position in this particular market not only for its immediate profit contributions but also for its "ripple effect" on other investment banking activities.[5]

In subsequent chapters, the analysis is broadened to incorporate some additional dimensions of competition which could be obscured by aggregate underwriting concentration data. The important transactional and counseling activities other than public financing range from capital structure planning and dividend policy advice to merger and acquisition and private placement assistance. These have long played important roles in the interaction between investment bankers and capital users, as the historical review in Chapter 1 indicates.

Chapter 3 treats in more detail the functions and competitive strategies of investment banks, to facilitate subsequent analysis of competition within the industry. Chapter 4 examines the client affiliations of a sample of 20 leading investment banking firms in an effort to identify explanatory patterns in the clusterings observed. Chapter 4 also examines the stability of these relationships over a sample period during the 1970s.

The client-banker affiliation patterns are then studied using logit analysis, a statistical technique. In Chapter 5 we attempt to discern the characteristics of each party that attract specific clients and investment banks to each other. In Chapter 6 we use the logit analysis to identify groups of investment banks within which competition for certain corporate clients is particularly vigorous. This effort helps to identify competitive submarkets within the larger investment banking industry. The concluding chapter summarizes the results of our investigation and offers some possible implications for the future.

1 Competition: A Historical Sketch

Investment banking in America evolved gradually out of the hodgepodge of financial services first available in the early 1800s. Viewed historically, the process by which these financial institutions developed both their relationships with clients and their methods of doing business reveals much about the industry's enduring dynamics of competition.

The development of investment banking owes much, of course, to local circumstances and influential personalities. Had there been no J. P. Morgan or Jacob Schiff, or had there been no need for railroad financing, the way that General Motors sells new equity would not be precisely what it is today. But it would not be all that different, either. What history makes clear is that the flow of capital through the hands of underwriters tends to seek out its own level.

Since the early 1800s, American investment bankers have managed the growing demand for capital through the use of underwriting syndicates. These syndicates have consistently taken on a pyramid-like shape and have been managed by the handful of firms at the pyramid's apex. Relationships of considerable loyalty and duration have existed between underwriting houses and client firms. In theory, pyramidal syndicate organizations, apex firms, and banker-client loyalty are not inevitable. In practice, they have been so. Something else—something more than the mere need to adapt to changing circumstances—has been at work.

The European Background

The European background of investment banking bears directly on its evolution in the United States. Although the interest of American banks in, for example, the retailing of securities in secondary markets was the product of market conditions in America, the transnational careers of individual bankers and joint ventures between European and American houses did help to shape financial services in America. More important for our purposes, the early course of developments in Europe offers an especially clear glimpse of the industry's underlying competitive dynamics at work.

The loan contractors. By the 1780s, England possessed a reasonably coherent market for public bills and securities. A genuine investor class existed, and subscriptions to public loans were generally open to limited combinations of wealthy private individuals and influential politicians. Within a decade loan contractors appeared who took on subscriptions in order to resell them at a profit. Heated discussions arose at the time as to whether (in Fritz Redlich's words) "the loan contractor was an independent link in a chain or a mere representative of [ultimate] subscribers; or, in other words, whether loan contracting was a business enterprise."[1]

The question was eventually settled: soon after the turn of the nineteenth century, even the wealthiest individual investors began to be crowded out of the original market for new subscriptions by the middlemen—James Morgan, Walter Boyd, the Barings, and Goldsmid and Co. are examples—with comparatively large pools of capital at their disposal. Direct government efforts to keep loan contracting competitive often produced the opposite of the result intended. For example, William Pitt's decision in 1784 to solicit public subscriptions to the government debt merely consolidated that debt in professional hands. Competition favored not the emerging investor class with its limited savings but rather the banking firms or partnerships with ample capital resources. These resources provided the large sums required for the initial purchase of securities and for stabilizing the market for their later resale.

To achieve their privileged standing, contractors often cooperated in putting together secret lists or embryonic syndicates for sharing the risks in a subscription bid. Although the use of lists was itself not new, their composition was. No longer limited to ultimate investors, the lists now included first the contractors and subcontractors and only then private individuals, who had to apply to the contractors for admission. The contractors negotiated the details of the loan, committed those whose names appeared on the list to the pledged amount of their subscriptions, assumed liability for the timely provision of the funds thus pledged, and stabilized the secondary market for loan securities against the manipulations of bearish stockjobbers.

Early investment bankers. English practice during this period developed somewhat apart from that on the Continent. Many of the families that would soon dominate English finance—the Barings, the Warburgs, the Rothschilds—were of European descent, and though there was some international cooperation, these cross-influences were not extensive.

On the Continent the need for public funds was still largely met out of the private resources of well-to-do individuals. But another financing mechanism was also in operation. A group of middlemen—among them the Gebrüder Bethmann in Frankfurt, and Hope and Company in Amsterdam—had appeared who "did not take shares in a subscription outright as did the English loan contractors ... [but] 'negotiated' whole issues on a commission basis ... [and then] disposed of the securities, with the sale of which they were charged, as fast as possible directly to capitalists, soliciting by letters, circulars, and advertisements."[2]

The wall between these Continental practices and English loan contracting was effectively breached in some of the major public financings after the Congress of Vienna in 1814–1815. In the process, Redlich argues, something legitimately called investment banking was born:

> Like the English loan contractors the early investment bankers took new security issues outright and not on a commission basis, as had done the Continental bankers. But, on the other hand, they dealt with complete issues, as had been customary on the Continent, and unlike earlier eighteenth-century loan contractors they did not compete with institutional or other ultimate investors for mere parts thereof. (To be sure, the English development was already turning in this direction after 1800.) Furthermore, although acquiring the issues

outright in English fashion, the early investment banks received a commission following Continental practice. Or to look at the matter from a different angle, the transactions corresponded to what would have been called "private subscriptions" in eighteenth-century England. But they differed from the latter in that only middlemen participated, i.e., bankers who meant to sell to speculators and ultimate investors and who received a commission.[3]

For Redlich, then, the point at which public financing crosses over into investment banking proper occurs when competition for new securities no longer exists "between direct investors and individual speculators, on the one hand, and loan contractors, on the other, the latter being defined as enterprisers who currently subscribe to new security issues in order to profit from resale."[4] Investment banking exists when ultimate investors abandon to professional middlemen the original market for new subscriptions.

The emergence of apex firms. The real significance of this departure of ultimate investors from the original securities market is that a mere handful of the most prominent investment houses came to dominate the flow of long-term capital into public securities. Heated competition did persist, however, among the smaller firms that desired to be included in the confederations or lists managed by the most influential firms.

What rapidly developed, in Redlich's phrase, was "some kind of oligopoly at the apex of the pyramid . . . supported by chains of middlemen."[5] Competition was not less fierce at the top of the pyramid than at its base. The threat of new entrants and of new alliances among established firms remained quite real. The risks involved in taking on major flotations could suddenly leave even the biggest firms badly exposed. When Walter Boyd, for example, who had dominated English loans during the mid-1790s, became overextended, the other members of his syndicate first reduced the size of his participation and then excluded him altogether. Similarly, the Barings were finally driven from their preeminent position by the Rothschilds. A break in the secondary price of the French *rentes*—probably engineered by the Rothschilds—had caught the Barings sufficiently exposed that they could save themselves only by canceling contracts and thus sacrificing their reputation.

The profits to be made from such flotations were so immense and the mutual benefit of maintaining discipline among syndicate participants in the flow of capital was so clear that the competitive pyramid was an indisputable fact by the 1820s. The early division of firms between the apex and the body of the pyramid was thus a natural outgrowth of competitive dynamics as they then existed. Ultimate investors had not yet developed into a diversified market, although the means for trading securities were already in place. The variety of financial products available to investors was not extensive. Loan participations differed, of course, in maturity, rate of interest, and degree of risk, but the loans themselves were relatively standard. The borrowers, sovereign states or their subordinate units, had—with the exception of wars and other emergencies—a predictable and recurring need for funds. In the early 1800s, even the demand for war loans had a certain regularity.

Although the universe of borrowers was quite small, the threat of their joining to dictate terms to the banking industry was largely offset by the endless political maneuvering among them. Their large financial requirements and the confidential "reasons of state" often underlying those requirements made timely access to capital and assurance of discretion essential. And these could be supplied only by firms able to "manage" the workings of the developing capital markets.

Indeed, the needs of governments virtually forced the emergence of apex firms and the discipline they were able to impose throughout the rest of the financial chain. But they ruled at a price: the erection of protective, though not impassable, barriers around the apex firms. Competition among them did not disappear but shifted from price to considerations of service: broad geographic access to capital, quality of service itself, reputation for reliability, proven ability to deliver as promised, and degree of control over a security's value on the secondary exchanges.

Then, as later, the industry's Achilles' heel was the availability of adequate capital. Because even the apex firms typically did not have the cash to meet their own loan repayments as they came due, they would often have to sell inventoried securities precipitously in the secondary markets. They would also borrow funds against the securities they kept in inventory, a practice that put them at the mercy of professionally bearish speculators. Only later would the Rothschilds teach the industry more advanced techniques of stabilization by actively orchestrating buying and selling activities on the various European exchanges to keep securities prices up.

American Developments to World War I

Developments in America lagged several decades behind those in Europe. Until the Civil War and railroad building of the mid-nineteenth century created ever increasing requirements for capital, financial services were provided by auctioneers and speculators, merchants like Stephen Girard and John Jacob Astor, brokers of every description, and incorporated commercial banks like Nicholas Biddle's United States Bank of Pennsylvania. By the 1840s, many providers of these services decided to become private bankers dealing in securities transactions. Some, like John E. Thayer and Brother, had originally been foreign exchange brokers; others, like Alexander Brown and Sons, had been merchants and shippers.

Influences from abroad. The American need for capital attracted representatives of such European houses as the Barings, the Rothschilds, and the Speyers. Alexander Baring, for instance, came over in person to work out the tricky financial arrangements for Jefferson's Louisiana Purchase. August Belmont, who quickly established his own banking operation, was initially an agent of the Rothschilds. Belmont retained close ties with them for many years, which in practice meant privileged access to their financial backing.

Soon thereafter, a number of German Jewish immigrants with commercial, if not directly financial, family backgrounds—most notably the Seligmans, the Lehmans, Abraham Kahn, Solomon Loeb, and Marcus Goldman—moved from assorted mercantile activities into private banking. Like such Yankee houses as Lee, Higginson and the several Morgan establishments in New York, London, and Philadelphia, the Jewish firms prospered because of their privileged access to European capital. Unlike the Yankee houses, however, they often enjoyed the business advantages of extensive family ties.

There were also numerous joint ventures between European and American firms. The Revolutionary era, of course, saw major efforts of short duration to raise money abroad. In the early nineteenth century, however, funding the public debt sent both government officials and commercial bankers like John Sergeant and Charles Wilkes to London, where they learned a great deal from the Rothschilds and the Barings about loan contracting and securities issues. In fact, until the post-1837 depression, London proved a most reliable source of capital for American needs. Some of these international alliances were temporary—domestic bankers trying to place small issues of local securities abroad. Others, like the association of Prime, Ward, and King in New York with the Barings, lasted even through the bleakness of the 1840s.

By the time Cooke & Co. failed, precipitating the great financial panic of 1873, the industry gave clear promise of its later development. Even though foreign buyers and large domestic institutions still absorbed the lion's share of new flotations, Jay Cooke's imaginative approach to selling government paper during the Civil War showed the value of aggressive sales tactics and a nationwide distribution system. It also identified the small individual investor as a potentially important dimension of the securities market. This attention to mass retailing had a distinctly American flavor. Loan subscriptions open to the public had enjoyed some success in Europe, especially France after 1850, but aggressive retailing found greater acceptance in America.

It was Cooke's genius to tap this universe of potential investors by establishing a nationwide, but centrally controlled, network of distribution agents and by supporting them with mass advertising. His appeals to patriotism helped, but earlier patriotic appeals without Cooke's retailing expertise had fallen on deaf ears. Cooke's grasp of the techniques needed to reach middle-class investors and his willingness to support the price of securities in the market defined the mix of salesmanship and stabilization characteristic of post–Civil War syndicates.

On balance, then, European influences transmitted a working knowledge of certain financial practices, and European houses controlled much of the later refunding of Civil War loans. They did not, however, have great effect on American investment banking structure or dynamics. Conditions general to underwriting activity and particular to the domestic U.S. market for securities counted for more.

Services and relationships. By the post–Civil War decade, the market for financial services was changing in important ways. Much in evidence, for example, was so-called active investment banking—banker influence (through membership on corporate boards or finance committees) upon the policies of client companies. In general, investment banking activity expanded by providing technical assistance with new issues and by supplying a wide array of financial advice and supporting services. As these involvements became more varied and extensive, longer-term loyalties between banker and client quite naturally emerged. These relationships, however, were based on more than familiarity.

Bankers' services, general financial advice, and reputation were highly enough prized that the client companies gradually came to encourage long-term alliances with selected investment houses— their "principal bankers." Although neither party was legally bound to maintain the alliance in the course of future flotations, as Vincent Carosso puts it,

> Close, continuous relationships between railroads and the investment houses that financed them, whether formal or informal, were encouraged by both bankers and railroad officials because both benefited from them. The banker's presence on the board facilitated sales of a road's securities; it gave investors confidence that their interests were being better served; and it appeared to constitute either an endorsement of the issue's "investment quality" or "practically guaranteed" it.[6]

For the bankers, relationships meant assured access to a substantial income, which in turn was necessary to attract and motivate the talented people who serviced the clients. As has been true throughout the history of investment banking, without unusually talented people to keep the banks flexible enough to meet new needs as they appeared, even established houses—like that of the Seligmans—could fall on hard times.

Still, bankers had innumerable ways to make money. There were fees for underwriting managements or participations, fees as registrar or transfer agent for securities, fees for financial consulting, fees for redeployment of a client's deposited funds, fees for overseeing consolidations or reorganizations, and fees for distributing security issues. However large the profits, the premier firms did not monopolize their industry. If anything, as flotations increased in size and retailing in importance, the leading houses relied more and more on the collaboration of second- and third-tier distribution firms around the country. As at virtually every stage of its evolution, investment banking exhibited an oligopolistic industry structure that was roughly pyramidal in shape, with a handful of powerful firms at the apex.

Leading houses like Morgan wanted to cement their own positions, but smaller establishments like N. W. Halsey & Co. found their own lucrative niches, as did nonapex commercial banks outside the eastern money centers. Local and regional issues often attracted the second- and third-tier firms, many of which also had a relatively open field in distribution operations. The flotations of utility companies did not typically appeal to the major houses, just as a generation or two later the flotations of retailers like Sears and of consumer-oriented light industries would not generate much apex interest. Kuhn Loeb, for example, had little use for industrial, as opposed to railroad, flotations until virtually the end of the nineteenth century.

The firms at the top of the pyramid did not try to compete in every niche of the market. Their strength lay in their ability to put together a group of investors—particularly institutional investors—more effectively than anybody else. As a result, they could absorb the risks of ever-larger flotations, remunerate the talented professionals who managed the services on which both profits and client loyalty depended, and move quickly whenever a new competitive opening was spotted.

As the resources of commercial banks, trust companies, and—most particularly—life insurance companies skyrocketed, institutions came to invest heavily in the securities issues managed by apex firms and quite understandably sought closer managerial involvement with them. These overtures were both welcomed and reciprocated. Officers of each of these various institutions typically owned the securities of the others or sat on their boards or finance committees. George W. Perkins, for example, was both a Morgan partner and chairman of the finance committee of New York Life Insurance Co. In 1913, as the Pujo investigations revealed, officers of five New York banks (Morgan, First National, National City, Bankers' Trust, and Guaranty Trust) held 118 directorships in 34 banks and trust companies, 30 directorships in 10 insurance companies, 105 directorships in 32 transportation companies, 63 directorships in 24 producing and trading companies, and 25 directorships in 12 public utility companies. Thus this group of men held 341 directorates in 112 companies having aggregate resources of $22 billion. The Morgan partners alone held 72 seats, and George F. Baker, Chairman of New York's First National Bank, personally held 58.[7]

With institutional cooperation assured, the trust companies, banks, and insurance companies benefited from the apex firms' reputation and influence as well as from a predictable supply of high-grade paper. For their part, the investment bankers enjoyed a more extensive and reliable supply of both short- and long-term capital. Even so, a single investment banking house could rarely by itself supply the money or absorb the risk involved in a major flotation. As a result, the use of formal syndicates became commonplace in all sorts of new-issues activity.

Conventions of syndicate organizations. The underwriting syndicates in which investment bankers participated had, according to Carosso, four historically distinct functions: (1) *origination,* the determination of the kinds, amounts, and terms of the securities to be underwritten; (2) *purchase,* the actual purchase of securities from issuer or originating house for distribution and resale; (3) *banking,* the provision by commercial banks of funds to purchasers, when resale was not quickly accomplished, so that they could keep obligations to issuers and originators; and (4) *sales and distribution,* the placement of securities with dealers or ultimate investors either on a straight commission or a contract basis. In practice, however, the first three functions were the responsibility of the originating house (or houses), usually an apex firm. This manager (or comanager) function stood clearly separate from the distribution function.

The managing firm had a number of distinct tasks and a wide range of discretion. It established the size and composition of the syndicate, formulated the terms governing origination and sales, determined the size of each member's participation, stabilized the issue's market price during the distribution and selling phases, enforced obligations and liabilities assumed by syndicate members, kept the syndicate's records, and passed out the syndicate's profits—for all of which it received a special manager's fee.

These arrangements represented an extension of earlier practice. Just as linkages grew between banks and their favored clients, so syndicate-based linkages grew among banks themselves. Inclusion in a syndicate—especially as a managing house— yielded the substantial profits and heightened prestige on which competitive success rested. Being asked to join a syndicate managed by others and, even more important, acquiring the power to ask others to join one's own syndicate dominated the attention of all investment banking houses.

The rules by which such offers were extended, though never really formalized, were broadly understood and generally followed. Sufficient financial strength and expertise to meet syndicate obligations were necessary, but they did not guarantee participation. The loyalties developed in a house's past relations with an issuer, if mutually satisfactory, were strongly considered in new flotations, as was the desire of managing firms to assure their own inclusion in future syndicates managed by others. According to one banker, "Participations in syndicates are given for the sake of getting participations in syndicates . . . [and are] taken for the sake of being able to offer participations in syndicates."[8]

These informal understandings, which were most often the product of simple oral agreement among what Jacob Schiff of Kuhn Loeb spoke of as a "circle of friends"[9] did not come without strings attached. A firm that did not meet its syndicate commitments or that sought inclusion only in the most profitable financings or that gained in any of a thousand ways a reputation for not pulling its own weight would quickly find itself left out of future arrangements.

"Every bank or banking house to whom we addressed the syndicate letter offering it participation in the syndicate," testified Morgan's partner Thomas Lamont, "has an absolute right to reject it."[10] Lamont did not, however, report on the generosity of spirit with which the House of Morgan would look upon the exercise of that right. As the *New York Times* asserted, "firms and individuals . . . cannot discriminate between promising and unpromising syndicates without being excluded altogether in the future.[11] In a financial universe that offered very attractive profits in return for being a responsible "member of the club," the rules may have been informal—a "matter of custom and business honor"[12]—but they were binding nonetheless.

This unspoken code provoked deep suspicion among the industry's critics. The specter of a few powerful houses controlling in secret and in seeming collusion the fate of American business could not help but stir up public suspicion. And these suspicions could not be allayed by simple assurances from leading financiers about their honorable behavior. The perception of a few apex firms sitting atop a pyramid of several hundred lesser ones and ruling them with the aristocratic strictness of an English public school headmaster was likely to create trouble. And, in the wake of the 1920s excesses, it did.

Some historians have argued that this public image implied a degree of competitive regimentation that did not in fact exist. The market for investment banking had become increasingly segmented after the 1870s, however, and the apex firms simply did not regulate competition in every market niche. Only a few of the larger houses (Lehman Brothers and Goldman Sachs, for example) interested themselves in the affairs of small, family-owned manufacturing or retailing companies. Still fewer bothered with municipal or local utility issues; most left those issues to aggressive regional houses. And as Carosso notes, "alert men [continually] organized new firms to meet local and regional needs and to cater to new investors with new services."[13]

But even in major corporate financings, the established houses differed in the services they provided and in their sources of profit. For instance, they varied considerably in the attention paid to establishing branch offices and to the retailing of securities. Kidder Peabody and Lee, Higginson jumped eagerly into such brokerage activity and used their retailing skills and distribution systems to win participations in syndicates run by confirmed wholesalers like Morgan and Kuhn Loeb.

The major houses no longer really had their chosen field to themselves. Substantial roles in new flotations went to the bond departments and security affiliates of commercial banks, as corporate deposits increasingly permitted them to act as institutional investors. Ambitious trust companies with liberal state charters also participated. In fact, access to investment capital anywhere throughout the country and to distribution systems able to tap that capital were sufficient means for new players to enter the industry. From a distance, the industry may have seemed relatively frozen in its disciplined commitment to "good form" and venerable custom; up close it looked more like a beehive of competitive activity—though a beehive in the shape of a pyramid.

Response to Conditions after World War I

Looking back on these developments half a century later, Judge Harold Medina in the early 1950s in *U.S.* v. *Morgan*—the antitrust case launched by the government against 17 major investment banking firms—put these changes in industry structure into perspective. It was, Medina contended, preposterous to assume, as the government prosecutors did, that these firms had first "entered into a combination, conspiracy, and agreement to restrain and monopolize the securities business of the United States" in or about the year 1915.[14] The industry had taken on modern form well before that. More important, this form—a pyramid with apex firms, and with the whole linked together by syndicate organizations—had been the basic shape of the industry at each stage of its development.

But neither this shape nor the position of firms within it had become frozen, Medina maintained. It was not a financial straitjacket, but represented the responses of countless individuals and institutions to certain recurring financial needs. It could, of course, be misused, but there was little sense in arbitrarily painting the whole with the broad brush of monopoly.

Medina reasoned that, because the flotation of a security issue was so complex, the process was not a standardized "it" that a few banking houses could monopolize. And because each issue was unique, bankers competed not by offering a commodity-like package of services at the lowest price but instead by trying to "establish or continue a relationship with the issuer," based on past performance, current reputation, and faithful adherence to the industry's informal code of conduct.

As a result, when speaking of competitors, "nothing but confusion will follow unless we first determine what is the 'it' for which the competitors are supposed to be competing." Put simply, Medina saw the industry pyramid as embodying a considerable amount of competitive activity because the "single, entire, unitary transaction" involved in a major underwriting is really the sum of many different banking services.[15]

Nor were these services "the product of accident or secret arrangement among the more powerful firms." They were, as Medina stressed time and time again, "the product of a gradual evolution to meet specific economic problems created by demands for capital, which arose as the result of the increasing industrialization of the country and the growth of a widely dispersed investor class." They were all "part of the development of a single effective method of security underwriting and distribution." In short, they represented over the years "the normal and natural re-actions of businessmen with common problems to the course of economic events." Even so, individual firms demonstrated a "con-spicuous lack of uniformity" in their manner of participation in the industry—or, in Medina's memorable phrase, a "pattern of no pattern."[16]

Though this conclusion may have been clear to Medina in re-trospect, it was not clear to the public in the first third of the twentieth century. Fears of an anticompetitive "money trust" rarely seemed to die down, and in fact were fueled by the gradual discovery not of secret plots or backroom collusion but of profes-sional incompetence, irresponsibility, and out-and-out fraud. Public reaction to the industry's gentlemen's club mystique had always been ambivalent. But following the great crash of 1929, public confidence in the system evaporated, as events continually gave the lie to the industry's reputation for sober and responsible management.

Along with this loss of reputation, the bankers no longer had vast discretion in their stewardship of the nation's private econ-omy. Revelations of stock waterings, bank mismanagement, and slipshod practices on the stock exchanges finally broke the terms of the long-implicit compact between bankers and society. Indus-try self-regulation was no longer enough. Demands for external regulation could no longer be avoided. A new legal order was needed—or so ran the social consensus—to police the industry's workings. But what that consensus did not foresee was that the arrival of explicit legal obligations would hasten the demise of an older, informal sense of personal and institutional responsibility. By 1930, no man or group of men had the acknowledged standing to do what Morgan had done to stem the Panic of 1907.[17] More to the point, few if any still felt the obligation to do so.

In such a climate, indictments of bankers' lack of probity went hand-in-hand with familiar accusations of excessive concentra-tion and banker control of industry. Although these new charges and the investigations they inspired occupied public attention, they often missed the significance of structural changes. First in New York and then in many other states, for example, life insur-ance companies were explicitly barred from further participation in underwriting syndicates and, in general, were forced to pull back from their close ties to various banking institutions—except, of course, as ultimate purchasers of securities. As a result, Carosso notes, syndicates became on average much larger than they had previously been, because it took many banking and brokerage firms to absorb the risk and amass the capital of a single insurance company. Syndicates therefore became more open to new entrants, and competition increased among old ones.

Partly in response to these developments, the established modes of syndicate operation began to feel new pressures. Financial houses outside New York started to raise technical questions about the way undistributed securities were divided among syndicate members. Also, as both syndicates and the flotations they managed grew larger, their life spans grew shorter and the arrangements among participating firms became more complex and more detailed. Selling syndicates (with either limited or unlimited liability) and selling groups came into wider use, but their members were very much at the mercy of originating houses.[18] The need to distribute a greater volume of securities more quickly than ever before—and at a greater distance from the origination process—diminished these firms' ability to know everything about the goods they sold. At the price of enforced ignorance, the firms found a niche for themselves in the industry. This compromise was by nature unstable, and the strain showed.

There were other noteworthy shifts in the industry's structure. As the speculative tide of the period spilled over into institutional changes, it carried all but the most conservative houses at least part way along. Kidder Peabody, for one, went rather far in this direction and paid for it dearly later on. Few private houses could resist altogether the blandishments of investment trusts or public utility holding companies, just as few incorporated banks could withstand the allure of security affiliates. In fact, by 1930 commercial and investment banks were handling roughly equal amounts of securities business. Fevered speculation in overpriced paper would, in retrospect, further tarnish the industry's reputation for sober good sense. It did, however, provide the opportunity for new or newly aggressive firms, like Halsey, Stuart and Blyth— many of them located outside the New York orbit—to become major issuing houses.

Fundamental changes were less conspicuous. With the prosperity of the 1920s the national appetite for securities became almost insatiable. Although the volume of stocks finally passed that of bonds in 1929 and the popularity of municipal and utility issues grew apace, there was still not enough sound product for the major houses to float and dealers to sell. Nationwide distribution networks appeared to sell what there was. Even a huge increase in the placements of foreign securities could not meet the clamorous demand.

Only for the handful of leading originating firms at the top of the pyramid did the post-1929 world continue to work pretty much as it had a generation before. Although the apex firms would be severely buffeted and some upset, in general they were able to keep if not their absolute, then their relative places—like corks in the ocean. For the rest, the world had in a sense turned upside down. No longer did supply drive demand. Market demand was now in the saddle and drove everything before it.

Glass-Steagall and Its Aftermath

In the 1930s a long history of suspicion and questionable behavior finally caught up with the investment banking industry. After years of functioning without stringent external regulation, the industry became, in the course of a decade, one of the most heavily regulated industries in the country. A variety of New Deal enactments—the Revenue Act, the Securities Act, the Securities Exchange Act, and of course the Glass-Steagall Act—wrought great changes. Yet when the dust finally settled, the resulting landscape had quite a familiar look about it.

Procedural revisions. Flotations now had to meet strict new standards of disclosure, and a waiting period separated the registration of an issue from its distribution. With only a few high-grade, low-risk issues to float, underwriting spreads declined and the need for elaborate multisyndicate participations fell off significantly. Originating houses continued to use their own retailing skills and passed the rest of the task along to commission-based selling groups, which had no underwriting responsibilities or liabilities. By and large, as one observer noted, syndicates now consisted of "a few large underwriting houses who sign the purchase contract with the issuer, dividing the liability in fixed proportions among themselves, and a far larger selling group which does no underwriting, the members receiving a substantial selling commission only for the securities actually sold by them."[19]

Although these developments were mostly evolutionary in nature, they created uncertainty and prompted both issuers and underwriters to protect their flanks. Underwriters insisted on pricing issues at the very last moment and on creating escape clauses for themselves if the market should turn sour, the issuer's standing turn doubtful, or the information in registration statements prove inaccurate. For their part, issuers began to turn to private placements as a way of getting around disclosure requirements, ensuring an immediate commitment for their securities, and speeding up the whole flotation process. As always, shifts in institutional procedure followed hard on the heels of environmental change.

Structural rigidities. But some institutional adjustments touched more than procedures. The Glass-Steagall Act, signed into law in June 1933, erected a barrier between investment and commercial banking. The Act had three objectives: discouragement of speculation, prevention of conflicts of interest, and promotion of bank soundness. Regarding speculation, the Act's proponents argued that if banks were affiliated with brokers, the former would have an incentive to lend money to customers of the latter. These customers might, in turn, invest their borrowings in securities rather than in what were believed to be more productive investments, such as hard assets. The conflicts of interest rationale hinged on the fear that commercial banks that had underwritten a firm's securities might then make imprudent loans to the firm to buttress the firm's financial structure while the bank had an equity interest. Perhaps most important was the soundness objective. Proponents of Glass-Steagall feared that banks' soundness could be threatened both by direct losses on securities held by a bank and by adverse effects on the public's confidence should a bank's securities affiliate falter. The Glass-Steagall Act was intended to respond to some of the glaring abuses that had encouraged, some thought, the bank failures and depression of recent years.

As a result of the Act's passage, established private bankers had to choose whether to give up their depository or their underwriting business; commercial banks had to sever relations with security affiliates and to scale down the activities of overgrown bond departments. Some firms disappeared. Others, including many small regional houses, emerged in a new guise. New firms appeared to occupy vacant niches. Morgan, for example, chose to keep its position in commercial banking, but several partners left to form the investment house of Morgan Stanley. The First Boston Corporation was patched together out of the cast-off security affiliates of several commercial banks.

Despite this flurry of organizational rearrangement, investment banking houses still provided much the same range of services as they always had. Indeed, the most significant result of the Act was that it froze investment banks out of commercial banking and commercial banks out of investment banking. Thus in effect it precluded entry into investment banking by a group of institutions that had formerly been among the industry's heartiest competitors—the commercial banks. Of course competition persisted, but it did so within an arena better safeguarded against intruders than ever before. And where entry was possible, lagging business conditions and the availability of capital through various New Deal agencies further narrowed industry spreads and made entry unappealing.

Within this protected arena, syndicates continued to function much as they had previously. The major firms on the scene by the late 1930s were, for the most part, composed of people and organizational units that had been parts of other firms before the mid-1930s. Since the complicated work of bringing securities to market still depended on close working relationships between bankers and issuers, new syndicate participations were still conditioned by past relationships. They were also conditioned by the financial competence and proven expertise—especially in distribution and sales—of individual houses. At the same time, however, newer forms of expertise—such as the provision of advice on private placements or on issues put up for competitive bidding—added significantly to the competitive repertoire of some firms.

On balance, therefore, a major effect of Glass-Steagall was to sharply curtail the natural entry of firms. Some established participants—the commercial banks, for example— were forced to leave the industry, much as the life insurance companies had been forced to leave in the wake of the Armstrong investigation a generation before. For the houses already in place and for the houses recently formed out of abandoned or disbanded institutional units, however, restrictions on the ebb and flow of competitors proved a boon.

Persistence of the pyramid. The sheer staying power of these competitive dynamics—even in the face of the important structural changes wrought by Glass-Steagall—argues strongly that the industry should be viewed along three different, though related, dimensions. The first is the various functions and services it provides. Considered in functional terms, the industry has remained virtually impervious to all outside forces—excepting, of course, the ever-present need to adapt to the changing financial requirements of the larger society. The second is the individual firms themselves. Here, too, the dominant impression is of constancy, with the unfolding evolution of the few great houses overshadowing the ceaseless comings and goings of other firms. Finally, there is the industry's institutional structure—the syndicate-based pyramid that has accompanied each stage of its evolution.

Typically, the industry's critics have lumped these three dimensions together, confounding their displeasure with specific houses with the inescapable dynamics of industry operation. When, for example, traditional banking relationships came under suspicion, more and more elaborate tests were designed to ferret out the lingering continuities between past and present firms that Glass-Steagall was to have abolished. Statistical data were used to show the persistence of a pyramid-like arrangement, which was dominated as before by a handful of apex firms. As Carosso observes, "in the four and a half years between January 1, 1934, and June 30, 1938, forty investment banking houses headed 94.2 percent of all managed issues in terms of value and held 82.6 percent in terms of value of all underwriting participations."[20] The real point, though, was not whether the pyramid still existed but whether it was being misused.

Even when, after the mid-1930s, rulings by the SEC and ICC required various classes of securities to be put up for public sealed competitive bidding, the pyramid organization of the bidding syndicates duplicated rather closely in form and in membership that of other underwriting syndicates. In fact, the decline in bankers' gross spreads, for which competitive bidding was more than a little responsible, hurt the small regional dealers it was designed to help by encouraging the larger houses to offset reduced spreads by doing more of their own securities retailing. Still, not all of the major firms leaped quickly into this field—Morgan Stanley, for example, did not—and not all of those which did were equally successful. Halsey, Stuart, according to Carosso, went from managing less than 1 percent of underwriting syndicates in 1940 to managing 29 percent in 1948, but that was quite unusual.[21] Thus, despite the hopes of its advocates, competitive bidding had as its major effect not a disruption of the pyramid but instead the gradual movement of some originating houses into permanent retail operations.

Investment Banking after World War II

The evolution of investment banking after World War II divides itself roughly into three phases. The first phase, which carried over into the first half of the 1960s, was characterized by unusual stability in the hierarchical structure. Two factors help explain the stability. First, as we have said, the Glass-Steagall Act, by barring commercial banks from participating in most aspects of underwriting, created barriers to entry that effectively excluded the best-positioned potential competitive entrants. Second, for a considerable period following the end of the war, the volume of underwriting and other corporate finance business was relatively stable—not rapidly growing—so that despite the apparent profitability of these activities the ground was not fertile for upward mobility among lesser firms in the investment banking hierarchy.

The essential sluggishness of capital markets until the mid-1960s, especially when combined with the protective barriers against new entrants raised by Glass-Steagall, did indeed help buffer the industry's structure from major change. Figure 1, which tracks the growth in dollar volume of corporate and municipal securities issues since 1934, shows only a modest—and uneven—upward trend before 1965. Much the same is true for the annual volume of shares traded on the New York Stock Exchange, another proxy for activity in the capital markets. Figure 2, which follows the data on share volume since 1934, shows a pronounced upward movement only after the mid-1960s.

For nearly twenty years after World War II, then, not enough new business existed to strain the industry's traditional pyramid structure, reinforced as it had been by the provisions of Glass-Steagall. Intrapyramidal competition at the apex—that is, the slow jockeying for position among established houses—continued, of course, at its normally unhurried pace. But this rate of adjustment

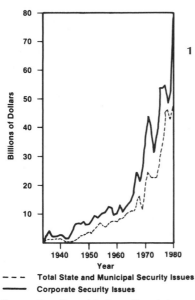

1 Dollar volume of securities issued, 1934–1980

Source—Securities and Exchange Commission

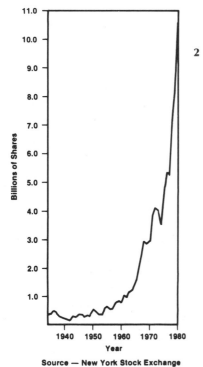

2 Annual share volume on the New York Stock Exchange, 1934–1980

Source — New York Stock Exchange

had never provided the driving force for substantial alterations in pyramid structure or in the relevant dynamics of industry competition. When such change had occurred, it had traditionally been fueled by the distributional skills and upward ambitions of the smaller houses below the apex. With minimal real growth in the volume of securities to be underwritten and retailed, therefore, these smaller houses had little on which to base such a move upward in the pyramid. Table 1, which lists for 1950–1980 (at five-year intervals) the top twenty investment banking houses in terms of the dollar volume of public offerings managed or comanaged, confirms this postwar state of affairs. Minor alterations in position do continually occur, but no substantial changes take place at the pyramid's apex. In fact, as table 1 indicates, six of the top eight firms in 1950 remained among the top eight firms three decades later.

In this environment the syndicate system—which had by then been refined into a very effective instrument for allocating risk and for managing distribution in public underwritings—also functioned as a de facto manager of the hierarchical structure of competition itself. A firm's relative position in the industry's pyramid largely determined its access to lucrative future business as well as to substantial current income. Standing was indicated not only by the frequency with which a firm managed or comanaged a major syndicate but also by the frequency of its participations in syndicates managed by others, the size of those participations, and the status and prestige following from them. In many ways, then, a firm's overall syndicate standing, which was most graphically expressed in the "tombstone" ads that appeared (and continue to appear) in the financial press, was a symbol of its real power in the industry.

The tombstone ads, like the pyramid they represented, divided syndicate members into several categories or, in the accepted phrase, "brackets." A few apex or special bracket firms—Morgan Stanley, First Boston, Kuhn Loeb, and Dillon Read—topped the list during much of this period and enjoyed the largest participations. Below this apex group came the "major bracket" and then the "major-out-of-order" firms, which had been granted major bracket status only provisionally. Last came several degrees of submajors, each with a relatively small participation but included primarily for their retailing abilities. If a firm's inclusion among the submajors depended on a good track record in distribution, elevation to major bracket status was far more complex. It rested upon such factors as the professional and, to a lesser extent, the social standing of the firm's partners, the firm's possession of an adequate capital base, its strength and staying power in distribution, and, perhaps most important, its ability to generate major business, which could be shared with other houses.

To receive the blessing of increased syndicate participations from the leading underwriting firms, other securities firms had in effect to add their support to its extant structure. Some tried more aggressively than others to exploit their competitive strengths and gain improved position. But this was the way syndicates and pyramids had always functioned, ever since their informal beginnings in late-eighteenth-century Europe. These mechanics represented no radically new phenomena. They were but the latest incarnation of a familiar set of institutional arrangements.

Up to the early 1960s, then, competitive dynamics remained pretty much as they had been, at least in outward appearance. Inwardly, however, something important had changed. Pyramid discipline, whose origins lay in the necessary mechanics and client loyalties of large-scale finance, had always received informal support. Among gentlemen, the code of responsible stewardship—though it worked to the advantage of apex firms—was worth supporting in and of itself. It was part of a system that merited willful adherence even from those to whom it offered only a modest share of the available benefits. Just after World War II the code, for the most part, still held. But developments were in the works which would alter that.

The ability of the syndicate system to maintain discipline within the investment banking business came under increasing pressure during the 1960s, a second phase in the evolution of postwar investment banking. A long economic expansion, accompanied by rapidly rising underwriting and secondary market trading volume, created conditions that allowed lesser firms in the pyramid to challenge the prevailing apex firms.

These lesser firms perceived that although the underwriting portion of Wall Street's total revenue stream was relatively small (approximately 10 percent for NYSE members in 1969, for example) it was also less cyclical, less burdened by heavy overhead, and in general much more profitable than, say, the retail brokerage end of the business. Nonetheless, the sustained profitability of these brokerage activities during the 1960s and the rapid rise in underwriting volume (see figure 1), which enhanced the value of distribution capacity to underwriting syndicates, worked to the advantage of several ambitious securities firms, allowing them to push their way into the apex group of syndicate leaders (see table 1). Among the most successful in moving up were Salomon Brothers and Merrill Lynch, both of which achieved their advance, at least in part, by exploiting their leading positions in areas of the distribution business. Salomon Brothers climbed from eighteenth place in the underwriting volume rankings in 1960 to fourth place in 1970. Merrill Lynch climbed only three notches during the same period—from fifth to second place—but its advance was very significant, having taken place at such a high level of the pyramid. As a result of their ascent, both Salomon Brothers and Merrill Lynch achieved the status of special bracket firms, initially in certain— and subsequently all—types of offerings. Meanwhile, as these and several other firms, including Goldman Sachs, ascended the hierarchy, they supplanted other firms whose declining fortunes resulted in demotion to a lower place in the pyramid. Halsey, Stuart, for example, fell from second place in 1960 to seventh place in 1970, and Kuhn Loeb fell from ninth to eighteenth.

In the 1970s, the third phase in the history of the postwar securities industry, there were other forces effecting change. Inflationary pressures exacerbated the high-volume "back office" pressures afflicting a number of the distribution firms, and a series of liquidations and mergers hit the brokerage sector of the industry. The introduction of negotiated brokerage commission rates in 1975 dramatically altered the economics of the brokerage business and precipitated another series of mergers and consolidations. In the same period, a new generation of finance professionals took over the reins from a generation more sensitive to institutional loyalties; challenges mounted to the informal discipline among and policing function of the apex firms; distribution capacity came to carry more weight in syndicate participations; foreign houses made themselves felt as a vital competitive force; institutional investors became a still more dominant part of the market; and corporate clients themselves became ever more sophisticated consumers of financial services. In short, the 1960s gave way to the 1970s, and established lines of demarcation within the industry grew weaker.

2 Trends in Concentration

Bearing in mind the historical continuity revealed by the preceding historical analysis, we now examine competition in investment banking in the 1970s. Our first step is to analyze trends in market share concentration, a statistic often employed to analyze an industry's competitive vigor.

This study focuses on concentration trends, during a period in the 1970s, in the large, relatively self-contained market for corporate negotiated public underwriting: *corporate* rather than government or municipal securities; *negotiated* instead of competitive-bid; *public* (that is, publicly offered) rather than privately placed securities; and *underwriting* (including origination, risk-bearing, and distribution) rather than secondary market brokerage, mergers and acquisitions, or other services. For reasons to be discussed below, alternative market definitions are less appropriate to use in analyzing competition. While other segments are not irrelevant to competition in corporate negotiated public underwriting, this market is a relatively distinct one. Many securities firms value a prominent position in this particular market not only for its immediate profit contributions but also for its "ripple effect" on other parts of investment banking.[1]

Corporate as opposed to municipal securities. Under the provisions of the Glass-Steagall Act, the general obligations of municipalities can be underwritten by commercial banks as well as by investment banks. This provision broadens the array of participants in municipal finance beyond the group of securities firms identified above.[2]

Negotiated as opposed to competitive-bid offerings. Part of the concern over concentration is the fear that one or more participants has or will gain a proprietary hold over an inordinate share of the securities industry business. Under competitive bidding, the underwriters of each successive offering of an issuer are chosen without regard to who underwrote previous financings; and management of a financing is largely a function of price competitiveness: market shares by industry participants tend to fluctuate significantly from year to year. While competitive offerings are thus excluded from our market definition, we will nonetheless analyze some of their concentration data to facilitate our analysis of the revenue-based concentration data later in this chapter.

Public offerings as opposed to private placements. Although corporate issuers frequently turn to private placements as an alternative to public offerings for raising new capital,[3] many types of financial institutions can service this market.

Domestic versus foreign. Within the corporate sector, foreign financings, which currently represent a modest part of the total financing activity,[4] can be looked at separately from domestic U.S. capital-raising efforts. Special skills and resources are needed to manage them, and the intermediary participants in the international market include a variety of commercial and merchant bankers in addition to U.S. investment bankers. Nevertheless, the importance of this market is growing, and in the concluding chapter of this book we shall address its possible impact on competition in the domestic corporate negotiated public market.

National as opposed to regional. A further refinement within the U.S. market identifies that group of corporate issues large enough to be of interest to national underwriting firms. For issues that fail to meet this size test, the relevant market may be a regional one, serviced by a relatively small number of locally based securities firms modest enough in size to undertake such financings profitably.

Concentration in the securities business has traditionally been measured by the dollar volume of managed or comanaged securities underwritten. This measure is thought to indicate the market power exercised by industry participants. The behavior of banking participants appear to support this view; for example, firms undertake considerable effort to propel themselves into leading positions with respect to total dollars of managed underwritings. Although management fees are often split equally among two or more comanagers, designation as the manager who will be "running the books" is highly valued for its superior client-contact position and its patronage control over the rest of the syndicate. Thus, industry listings of banks' financing volume often award a special bonus volume credit to the lead manager of a syndicate to recognize the special value of exercising control over the disposition of underwritten securities.[5]

In our analysis of concentration data, we have made an effort to discriminate between bona fide time trends in concentration and those movements which reflect a recurring, consistent relationship between volume fluctuations and concentration. Initially, the data were examined to discern such patterns; then they were tested for the relative importance of time trend and volume fluctuations in simple regressions.

Concentration is measured using two types of data: (1) the dollar volume figures on securities issued in each year for which the bank was either the lead manager or a comanager, and (2) the bank's annual revenue from underwriting activities (the combination of origination, underwriting, and distribution). The sample period for dollar volume is 1972–1977. The sample period for underwriting revenue data is 1970–1977. These years encompass a period of substantial upheaval and change in the securities industry. Dollar volume figures are reported first, followed by revenue data.[6]

For both sets of concentration data, our universe comprises the top 25 underwriters. This means that when we speak of total volume we really mean the total volume underwritten by the top 25 banks. And when we speak of total revenue we mean the total revenue earned by the top 25. Thus the concentration ratios we report are fractions of these totals, not of the totals for the entire securities industry. This simplification is satisfactory for our purposes because the top 25 underwriters include almost all of the nationally competitive investment banks. We should also mention that our volume figures give full credit to all comanagers of an offering. Thus there is some double counting, and the sum of the volumes of underwriting with which each firm is credited exceeds the true volume of securities the 25 banks underwrote in the period.

Volume of Financings

A visual inspection of the summary data in tables 2–4 and figures 3–11 suggests that, using volume as the relevant measure, concentration did indeed increase over the period 1972–1977. Although the results are somewhat muddied by year-to-year shifts, table 2 shows that shares of combined negotiated corporate equity and debt offerings held in 1977 by the top 4 (52 percent) and the top 8 (74 percent) were higher than the 42 percent and 66 percent shares held at the beginning of this period. Market share of the top 15 showed a modest but discernable trend toward increased concentration in the first half of the sample period (91 percent in 1974; 85 percent in 1972).

A separate examination of negotiated debt and equity yields further insight. Table 2 suggests an increase in concentration for *negotiated corporate debt* between 1972 and 1977 for the top 4 (43 percent to 52 percent) and the top 8 (68 percent to 74 percent). Because the total market share of the top 15 was essentially unchanged, market shares within that group obviously changed, particularly to the advantage of the top 4 participants.

The concentration trend suggested by table 2 is even more unambiguous in *negotiated corporate equity* underwritings. During 1972–1977, the market shares all appeared to increase substantially for the top 4 (39 percent to 50 percent), the top 8 (58 percent to 74 percent), and the top 15 (79 percent to 93 percent). This shift indicates not just a shuffling of market shares among the larger market sector participants, but also a significantly increased concentration of market power among this group, at the expense of others.

While these data do suggest a trend toward increased concentration, the graphs in figures 3, 4, and 5 also seem to show a tendency for concentration to increase when aggregate volume (for all banks) falls and to decrease when volume rises. Thus at least some of the "trend" in concentration may result from temporary dips in total volume during the sample period. If that is true, then a reversal in the downward volume trend will reverse (or partially reverse) the assumed trend toward concentration.

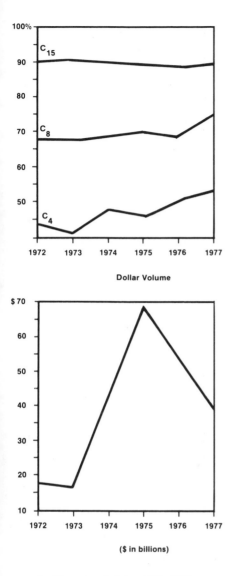

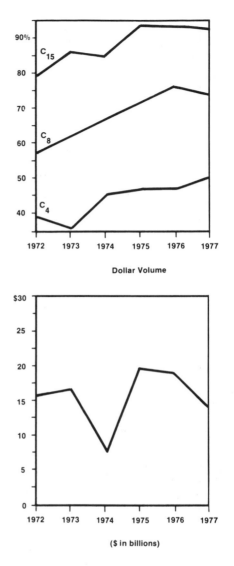

3 Negotiated debt, 1972–1977
   dollar volume concentration

4 Negotiated equity, 1972–1977
   dollar volume concentration

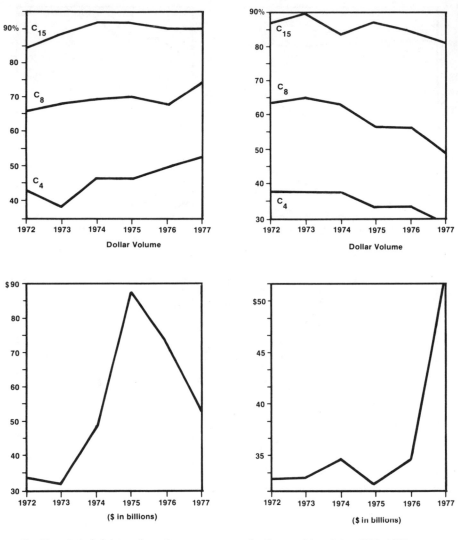

5   Negotiated debt and equity,
    1972–1977
    dollar volume concentration

6   Competitive debt, 1972–1977
    dollar volume concentration

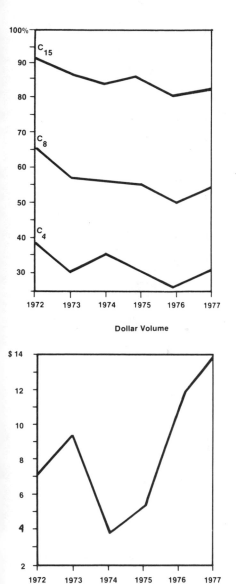

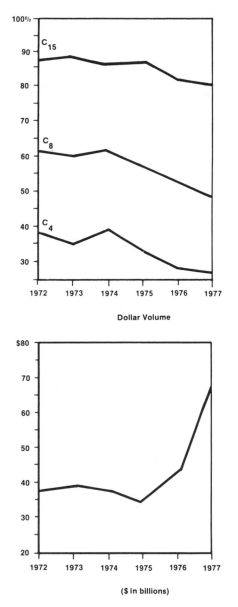

Dollar Volume   Dollar Volume

($ in billions)   ($ in billions)

7 Competitive equity, 1972–1977
    dollar volume concentration

8 Competitive debt and equity,
    1972–1977
    dollar volume concentration

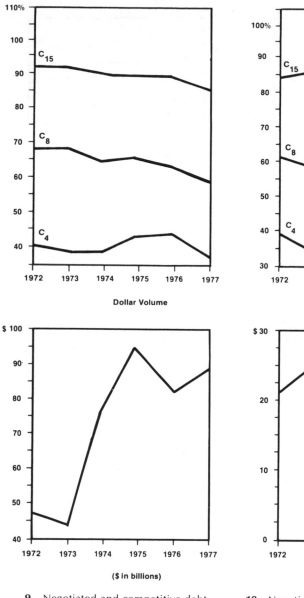

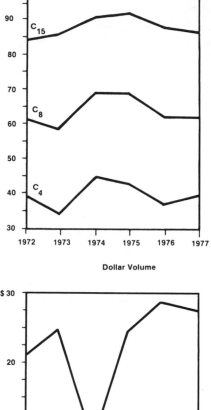

Dollar Volume

Dollar Volume

($ in billions)

($ in billions)

9 Negotiated and competitive debt, 1972–1977 dollar volume concentration

10 Negotiated and competitive equity, 1972–1977 dollar volume concentration

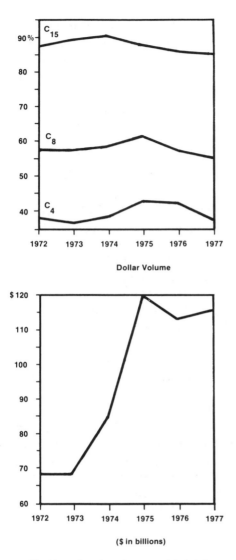

Dollar Volume

($ in billions)

11 Negotiated and competitive debt
and equity, 1972–1977
dollar volume concentration

In an attempt to sort out these conflicting observations, we regressed concentration on both time and dollar volume for each category of securities. The regression results set forth in table 5 confirm the contention that there is indeed a longer-term secular trend toward concentration. For both the negotiated debt and equity categories time generally has a positive and significant coefficient.[7] For fluctuations in concentration ratios caused by shifts in aggregate *volume*, the coefficients are insignificant for both negotiated debt and equity. No volume-concentration relationship is in evidence to obscure the observed secular trend toward increased concentration.

For the purposes of subsequent comparisons with revenue data, we collected and analyzed similar data on the competitively underwritten debt and equity categories (see table 3 and figures 6, 7, and 8). The regression results, presented in table 3, indicate that whereas the negotiated sector was undergoing a secular trend toward increased concentration during the test period, the opposite was occuring in the competitive sector. Competitive debt has a negative and significant coefficient and competitive equity produces test results that are inconclusive although negative in their sign; this indicates a secular decline in concentration at the same time that the negotiated sector was exhibiting increased concentration.

When negotiated and competitive data are aggregated (see table 4 and figures 9, 10, and 11), the *combined debt* regression has a negative and significant coefficient (that is, suggesting a secular decline in concentration) (see table 5). The *combined equity* regression has a positive but marginally significant coefficient (suggesting a secular increase in industry concentration), reflecting the greater weight of the negotiated volume in the combined total.

Revenue from Underwriting Activity

While dollar volume figures (and more specificially the negotiated part) are helpful in measuring concentration, they are not necessarily a complete picture of the industry's competitive vigor. Dollar volume figures only measure the purported *control* over public financing. They do not indicate how the ultimate profits from the activity are actually dispersed among various competing securities firms. It can be argued that another important measure of market dominance is the extent to which the actual spending power from the gross spread compensation for the intermediary role is retained by a small group of powerful securities firms.[8]

This annual aggregate gross spread revenue directly measures (1) the firm's management fees for originating financing deals, (2) fees for the firm's share of the underwritten guarantee to the issuer, (3) selling concessions for securities sold by the firm (the firm as manager can influence how many securities it will retain for its own in-house sales), and (4) the underwriting fees and selling concessions earned from reciprocal inclusion in the financing syndicates managed by other firms.

Although the revenue approach to measuring concentration has not to our knowledge been used effectively heretofore, that may have been due to the absence of publicly available data on underwriting income. We were able to gain access to some SEC gross spread revenue data for 1970–1977. These data, however, are not separated into negotiated and competitive-bid offerings. Thus, one must be particularly careful in interpreting the results of an aggregate statistical analysis. Tables 6 and 7 and figures 12, 13, and 14 present the data and test results.

In table 6 and figure 14, a visual inspection of the trend in combined debt and equity revenue distribution for the period 1970–1977 suggests significantly greater concentration in each of the top four, eight, and fifteen categories over the sample period. When this composite is broken into its debt and equity components, the discernible trend toward concentration in the corporate debt area (figure 12) does not appear to be matched in corporate equities (figure 13).

A year-to-year comparison also suggests that total revenue and industry concentration tend to move in opposite directions. Perhaps, as we had earlier hypothesized for financing volume figures, changes in concentration are better explained by the level of underwriting activity (as reflected in the total revenue data) than by a time trend. Thus, during periods of relatively high volume, concentration in revenue receipts would tend to decline; during slack underwriting periods, it would increase.

As with the earlier dollar volume data, we attempted to test these visual observations by regressing concentration on volume of business done and on time. A positive relationship with time

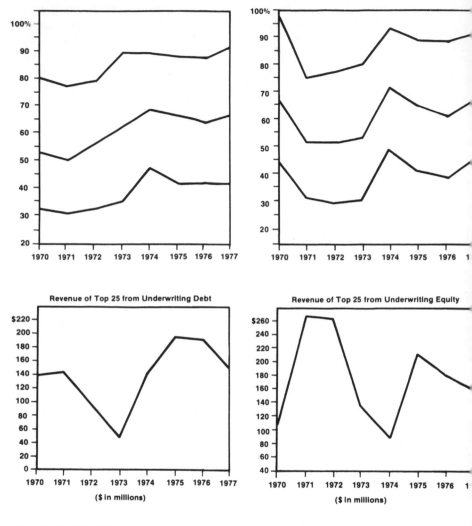

Revenue of Top 25 from Underwriting Debt

Revenue of Top 25 from Underwriting Equity

($ in millions)

($ in millions)

12   Debt, 1970–1977
revenue concentration

13   Equity, 1970–1977
revenue concentration

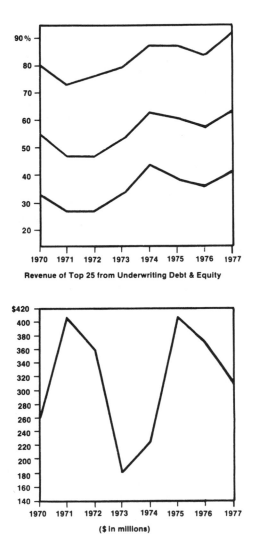

Revenue of Top 25 from Underwriting Debt & Equity

($ in millions)

14 Debt and equity, 1970–1977
revenue concentration

would indicate a clear trend toward increased concentration of the gross spread benefits of underwriting activity. On the other hand, correlation with level of revenue would suggest that concentration changes were responses to fluctuations in the year-to-year revenue from financings.

More specifically, for each annual total of debt revenue, equity revenue, and total revenue, and for each of the concentration ratios for four, eight, and fifteen firms, we regressed concentration on time and on the relevant total revenue figure. If concentration is measured in terms of revenue from issuing debt, the revenue figure used as an independent variable is total debt revenue. Similarly, total equity revenue is used in the equity calculations. The results are reported in table 7.

In the case of debt, the statistical results confirm a secular trend toward increased concentration. The time coefficient is both positive and significant. The volume coefficient is generally not significant. In the case of equity, the time coefficients are not significant although they are positive in sign. Moreover, the volume coefficients are generally negative and significant.

Interpretation of these revenue regressions for their implications for the negotiated underwriting sector must be approached carefully. It is noteworthy that, in regression on time, negotiated dollar volume of debt and combined negotiated and competitive debt revenue both have positive and significant coefficients. This indicates that in the debt sector the underwriting leadership is secularly growing more concentrated over time and that, concurrently, a larger proportion of the gross spread revenue is being retained by a relatively small number of securities firms.

In the case of equity, the time results are more equivocal. The positive and significant statistical result noted earlier with equity financing volume is supported here by a positive but ambiguous result with combined equity revenues. The fact that the combined revenue sign is positive even though the competitive equity volume sign is negative and significant suggests that if we were able to separate out negotiated revenue alone its sign would also be positive and significant. Thus, our findings suggest a secular trend over time toward increased concentration of gross spread revenues from negotiated equity underwriting.

With respect to coefficients for total revenue, the statistical tests for both negotiated debt financing volume and combined debt revenue produce inconclusive results, thus providing no evidence that there is any relationship between levels of revenue and concentration at work in the debt sector.

In the combined equity sector, recall that the results of the regression of concentration on financing volume were inconclusive, although the sign was negative in the competitive sector alone. The fact that the combined equity revenue sign is negative and significant suggests the possibility that in the negotiated sector, but even more likely in the competitive sector, there is indeed a particular pattern in the way the revenues for underwriting activities are distributed among industry competitors. We conclude, then, that there is an inverse relationship between revenue concentration and total revenue in the equity area, with a greater concentration during periods of low activity and greater revenue dispersion during high-volume years.

There are several possible explanations for this inverse relationship. Smaller and usually more marginal issuers tend to drop out of the public offering markets during slack periods identified with economic slumps and with more quality-conscious investor sentiments. These second-tier-quality issuers are principally associated with the smaller investment banks.[9] The larger, more powerful investment banks tend to be associated with the larger, first-tier-quality corporate issuers, who usually have continued access to the public markets even during recessions.[10] Even in the competitive area, the largest issuers tend to attract bidding syndicates headed by one or more of these leading underwriting houses. This behavioral pattern would account for temporarily increased concentration among the leading underwriting firms during downturns.

Alternatively, it may be that all types of underwriting activity decline proportionately during downturn periods but that the larger, more powerful underwriting houses compete more aggressively for the available business (even for lower-quality business) and, particularly, for competitive-bid underwritings.

A third possible explanation postulates that during slack periods the leading firms sell a larger fraction of their securities through their own distribution systems in order to preserve for themselves the lucrative selling concessions from the gross spread. Given their heavy quasi-fixed cost structures, the pressures for leading firms to follow this pattern could be compelling during years in which revenues from other sources decrease.

In sum, there is some evidence of a secular increase in concentration in the underwriting part of the securities business during the period covered by our study. It is most evident in the negotiated debt sector. While there is also statistical evidence of increased concentration in equity financing volume, the statistical results are equivocal with respect to equity revenues. At the same time, however, there is evidence of a statistically significant inverse relationship between total revenue and concentration, although utilization of combined negotiated and competitive underwriting revenue data makes the drawing of inferences regarding the negotiated portion more difficult.

While these concentration findings are not inconsistent with patterns observed at various points in the historical evolution of the pyramidal structure of investment banking articulated in Chapter 1, they are not sufficient as a description of actual competition within the pyramid or of the degree of stability in the positions of leading apex firms. The underwriting–corporate services market is not homogeneous. The services of the competitors are differentiated; the needs of clients vary. These observations and others underlie a rising level of skepticism among both theorists and practitioners about the reliability of concentration data as a definitive measure of the robustness of competition in an identifiable industry segment.[11] In effect, these observers argue that one must explore each industry in detail to understand the factors which add to or detract from competitive vigor. It is with this in mind that we turn in succeeding chapters to a more in-depth look at competition within the classic investment banking industry.

3 Functions and Strategies of Investment Banks

In any industry there are groups of firms with relatively similar competitive strategies and market niches. Categorizing the groups is one way of analyzing the structure and competitive forces within the industry. In this chapter we introduce a functional model of competition in investment banking and examine the extent to which barriers to entry or mobility are present within the industry. We focus in particular on a group of twenty firms drawn from among the industry's underwriting leaders. Several other firms of growing importance (such as Donaldson, Lufkin and Jenrette) were omitted because their rise has been too recent to be encompassed by our sample period.

Firms' competitive profiles may differ along any of a number of dimensions:

Participation in and share of various market segments

Breadth of product line

Quality of product(s) or service(s)

Other differentiating characteristics of products, such as customer services, the nature of the distribution system, etc.

Degree of vertical integration

Financial structure

Corporate goals and objectives

Corporate diversification into related or unrelated businesses

Customer base

The firms' differences along these dimensions will affect their behavior, their costs, and their profitability. These characteristics thus provide a basis for understanding the market's competitive structure and predicting the most likely direction of any future change. We now turn to a presentation of these characteristics as they apply to the investment banking industry.

Definition of Service Functions

As the historical survey in Chapter 1 revealed, in investment banking—or, more accurately for our purposes, in the corporate negotiated public underwriting market—firms perform several relatively distinct services:

Originating and managing a new financing issue involve determining the security's issue price, timing the issue, and recruiting the firms that will distribute the securities. Closely related to issue management is the provision of corporate financial services, ranging from consulting on corporate capital structure to advice on mergers and acquisitions.

Underwriting involves absorption of the risk assumed when the underwriter contracts to purchase an issuer's securities at a fixed price in spite of the uncertain price at which the securities can be reoffered to investors. (The term "underwriting" is often used to refer to all three public financing services: origination, risk taking, and distribution.)

Distribution involves selling the securities to the ultimate holders. Distribution divides naturally into two parts: distribution to institutional investors and distribution to individuals. Distribution is usually, though not always, performed by firms that are also active brokers or principals in the secondary corporate securities markets (that is, in buying and selling previously issued corporate securities). These secondary markets service the liquidity needs of investors and provide the underwriter with up-to-date information to aid in pricing a new issue. The secondary-market function could alternatively be categorized as a separate, fourth service performed for corporate clients as a component of the maintenance of access to the public capital markets.

In earlier chapters we established that investment banking firms differ significantly from one another in the degree of their participation in these three services, including the secondary-market brokerage function. The vertical and horizontal dimensions of the activities of investment banking firms can be listed as follows:

Financing activity	Related services and markets
Origination	Corporate finance services
Underwriting	Corporate finance services
Distribution	Secondary market
	Brokerage
	Institutional
	Retail
	Market making
	Arbitrage

The public capital-raising services we have identified—origination, underwriting (the bearing of risk), and distribution—can be thought of as the three vertical components of underwriting. The right-hand column of this list shows closely related activities that usually accompany a vertical piece of the underwriting process. Origination firms generally provide a variety of corporate finance services, such as merger advice, that strengthen the link between the investment bank and the corporate client. Any firm that distributes underwritten securities almost always has a secondary-market operation, since the volume of newly issued securities alone will not usually support an organization capable of distributing them.

In any study of investment banking, it is particularly important to understand the vertical dimension of the market. While most major investment banks are active in all three vertical segments, their strengths in each segment vary considerably from firm to firm. Thus, some firms primarily originate issues, carry out related corporate finance services, and undertake various services for the primary and secondary institutional market. Others serve as secondary-market brokerage firms whose major strengths lie in distribution; they do only a modest amount of origination and related corporate service work.

The investment banking spectrum includes firms at these extremes and at many points in between. A central issue concerning competition is how the different areas of strength influence client choices of investment banks and, therefore, affect the competitive behavior of those banks and the evolution of the industry structure over time.[1] The Securities Industry Association (SIA) has developed a classification scheme for investment banks which is broadly congruent with the alternative firm characteristics discussed above. It labels one group as "large investment banking firms," whose primary emphasis is on underwriting and related functions. A second category, "national wirehouses," describes firms with a national retail distribution capability and a major preoccupation with this market niche. Other categories include various types of specialized and regional securities firms.[2]

All of the firms included in our group of twenty top participants in corporate negotiated underwritings fall into the first two of these classifications.[3] Table 8 presents the list, with the "large investment banking" group further subdivided into "special bracket" and "other." The "special bracket" designation is an industry-initiated recognition of special market power possessed by five leading securities firms by virtue of their strong corporate client bases and/or their unique skills in distributing securities and maintaining markets.[4]

Internal Barriers to Mobility

Certain barriers to entering the U.S. securities industry—principally the Glass-Steagall Act discussed in Chapter 1—have impeded the encroachment of competitors from outside the industry. Other important impediments may affect the ability of securities firms to move between the groups discussed above.

As the previous discussion suggests, we can divide the securities underwriting activities of investment banks into several parts, including origination and (institutional and retail) distribution. Considerable evidence suggests that securities firms can move into the institutional brokerage and market-making area if they are willing to commit the necessary people and financial resources.[5] Moreover, the statistical results of past studies suggest that the retail brokerage business involves only modest economies of scale at the local level, so that, historically, no insuperable barriers to entry exist here.[6] Entry into and continued maintenance of retail distribution at a large enough scale to be competitively useful in underwriting at the national level may still be difficult to achieve.

Important barriers appear to inhibit entry into the corporate finance–origination segment. They center on the difficulty of acquiring the reputation, quality of resources, and amount of client loyalty that characterize the successful firms. To support the hypothesis that the principal barrier to internal mobility in investment banking lies in the corporate origination area, it is necessary to show that (1) securities firms without a historical participation in underwriting leadership (that is, primarily the retail distribution firms) have made efforts in that direction, and (2) despite those efforts, they have not been successful in dislodging—or at least sharing substantially with—the well-established leaders in the available underwriting–corporate finance business.

The evidence suggests that many of these national wirehouse firms have in fact worked substantially to expand their origination activities. In addition to the firms' stated intentions to compete more aggressively in origination,[7] several statistics indicate the impressive manpower and financial resources they have committed to this effort. Table 9 shows the numbers of professionals added from 1965 to 1978 by a sample of securities firms drawn from both the large investment banks and the national wirehouse categories. Table 10 documents a sample group of firms' investments in regional corporate finance offices, the overhead burden for which is usually substantial. By either reckoning, the aspiring retail distributors have in recent years made substantial investments to generate momentum in the underwriting–corporate finance business.

Comparative dollar volume statistics suggest that the aspirants have not, on the whole, met with a great deal of success in this expansion effort. Although several securities firms have exhibited significant progress, table 11 shows that essentially those originators that dominated at the beginning of the decade also dominated at the end of it, when market share is measured by volume of lead managerships. The analysis in Chapter 2 also suggests that the negotiated underwriting business was, if anything, becoming even more concentrated among the leading firms during much of the decade of the 1970s.

However, the proportion of financings utilizing one or more comanagers has increased in recent years (table 12). Further, an examination of *Institutional Investor's* directory of client-bank affiliations over a period of years also suggests some fragmentation of the closely held client core, as the number of such affiliations has grown substantially. Finally, the trade press has run numerous articles and news items in recent years chronicling the increasingly ad hoc attitude toward investment banking relationships being adopted by corporate issuers on each successive piece of business. Thus, an analysis of the determinants of these bank-client relationships seems in order.

4 The Major Investment Banks and Their Client Bases

In this chapter we analyze in detail the client bases of specific investment banks as an aid to understanding the industry's contemporary competitive structure. For a group of 20 top investment banking firms (as measured by leadership in negotiated underwriting volume in recent years), we have assembled data on the firms' clients among the *Fortune* top 500 industrial companies and among the top 50 transportation companies, banks, nonbank financial services firms (hereinafter called "diversified financials"), retailing firms, and utilities.

This analysis required selecting a criterion for determining which corporations were "clients" of each bank. The client relationship is sometimes difficult to define; naturally, considerable dispute arises in the industry about which companies can properly be called clients of which banks. In this book we apply and compare the following two criteria:

1. The *Institutional Investor* criterion. In *Institutional Investor*'s 1979 "Who's With Whom" tabulation, an investment bank was credited with having as a client each company for which the bank had (a) managed the company's most recent public offering or arranged the company's most recent private placement—whichever was more recent; (b) acted as dealer-manager in a tender offer; (c) provided advice on a merger transaction; or (d) acted on a fee basis. Test a was applied only to transactions that had taken

place within the preceding five years. Tests *b, c,* and *d* were probably applied to the same period, but *Institutional Investor*'s explanation of its tests does not make this clear, and at the time of this writing *Institutional Investor* could not confirm the period used. Each successive test was applied if and only if the preceding tests identified no investment banks. No investment bank was credited with having as a client a company that requested that no investment banks be listed.[1]

2. The lead manager criterion. According to this criterion, an investment bank was credited with having as clients all and only those companies for which it had been the lead manager of a public offering during the five years 1974–1978.

The *Institutional Investor* criterion, since it takes account of comanagerships and private placements as well as lead managerships, represents a fairly broad test for client-bank affiliations. The lead manager criterion, by contrast, is more restrictive, acknowledging a client-bank affiliation only where the bank was designated to "run the books" on a public offering.

Neither of these two approaches is completely satisfactory or definitive. The *Institutional Investor* criterion is controversial and, to some extent, subjective. Indeed, a number of investment bankers take strong issue with some of the assignments made.[2] The lead manager criterion is not open to the same dispute as to assignments, but because it does involve a narrower, more restrictive definition of the banker-client relationship, it is also subject to misinterpretation. For instance, it risks including as a bank's client a company that no longer has any relationship with the bank. In the end, however, the statistical results produced using the two different approaches were generally congruent.

Client Size and Perceived Quality

At the outset it was necessary to separate out general characteristics of client bases that would discriminate by both client size and perceived quality of credit risk. The *Institutional Investor* list analysis in table 13 shows an interesting discrimination with respect to size of corporate industrial client as measured by sales, profits, and net assets. Morgan Stanley enjoys a substantial lead over any other firm, followed by Salomon Brothers, Goldman Sachs, and, curiously, Dean Witter with its small eight-client base in the industrial sector. Retail-oriented firms such as Bache, E. F. Hutton, and Paine Webber, by contrast, tend to cluster at the lower end of the scale of sales, profits, and asset size.

When lead managers are used as the discriminating criterion, Morgan Stanley is again highest in terms of clients' magnitude of sales, profits, and net assets. It is followed by firms such as Blyth Eastman, Dillon Read, First Boston, Goldman Sachs, and Lehman Brothers. Using the lead manager criterion, the retail firms again tend to cluster toward the lower end of the scale of client size.

A similar but less distinct pattern emerges from table 13 with respect to characteristics designed to identify a client's perceived quality as a credit risk. The most straightforward measure, bond rating, is illuminating. Morgan Stanley's average bond rating (a little below a double A) is the highest, closely followed by originating firms Salomon Brothers, Dillon Read, Lazard Frères, Goldman Sachs, and Smith Barney. At the lower end are Bache, Bear Stearns, Drexel Burnham, E. F. Hutton, Loeb Rhoades, and Warburg, all firms more closely associated with the retailing part of the distribution business.

Another potential measure of quality—significant institutional holdings of a client's equity shares—gives less insight. It is difficult to distinguish at all at the high end. At the low end, we note the lowest average institutional holdings are attached to clients of retail-oriented Bache and E. F. Hutton; however, other retail firms have substantial institutional holdings among their clients.

From this analysis of client quality and size, it can be said in summary that the data at the end of 1978 give some evidence that the historically well-established group of apex firms did indeed have client bases that were larger and of somewhat higher perceived quality than those of the national wirehouse group.

Market Shares of Specific Industry Groups

Next we examine investment banks' client bases by industry categories, to see to what extent the well-established originators enjoyed leading positions in specific market segments.[3] Initially we employ six broad categories used by *Fortune* magazine in its annual compilations (industrials, commercial banks, diversified financials, retailing, transportation, and utilities); later in the chapter the industrial category is broken down into smaller components. Table 14 presents the results using the *Institutional Investor* criterion; table 15 uses the lead manager criterion. The following discussion covers some of the significant insights drawn from these data (for a more detailed analysis of the findings, see Appendix A).

Looking first at aggregates, we see that those firms with 6 percent or more of the total corporate relationships at the end of 1978 (using the *Institutional Investor* criterion) constituted essentially the same group of apex firms that had historically led in underwriting volume over the previous decade: Blyth Eastman, First Boston, Goldman Sachs, Kidder Peabody, Lehman Brothers, Merrill Lynch, Morgan Stanley, and Salomon Brothers. When the lead manager criterion is substituted, Blyth Eastman and Kidder Peabody drop out of the group, leaving only the special bracket firms and Lehman Brothers.

Essentially the same group of originators reappears when the aggregates are broken down into the six *Fortune* components using either the *Institutional Investor* or the lead manager criterion. Some relative strengths in specific industry categories are notable. Among commercial banking and diversified financial companies, for example, Salomon Brothers was prominent, possibly reflecting in part its historical role in this market sector. Similarly, Goldman Sachs' and Lehman Brothers' large proportion of the client relationships in the retailing sector may stem in part from their own merchant origins and their long-time advisory roles to leading U.S. retailers. Predecessor firm Kuhn Loeb's highly successful capital-raising efforts on behalf of various U.S. railroads, dating from the late 1800s, may help explain the prominence of Lehman Brothers in the transportation sector. Utilities' need for frequent infusions of capital and the importance of retail investors as target buyers of these securities may help account for Merrill Lynch's strong showing in the utilities sector.

Concentration ratios for bank-client relationships in these various categories are summarized in table 16. Under the *Institutional Investor* criterion, more than half the relationships in most categories were held by a group of four top firms and more than 80 percent were held by a group of eight top firms. According to the lead manager criterion, with the industrials excepted, the top four and the top eight firms respectively held about two-thirds and 90 percent of the relationships. It is interesting to observe that retailing and commercial banking appeared to be the most highly concentrated, using either assignment criterion, and that industrials were the least concentrated.

The industrial sector is of particular interest, since it accounts for almost two-thirds of the corporate relationships in our sample. Again, the already identified leading originating firms were typically dominant. Under the *Institutional Investor* criterion, the six leading firms were Goldman Sachs, Merrill Lynch, Lehman Brothers, Morgan Stanley, First Boston, and Kidder Peabody. Under the lead manager criterion the list is the same, though the order changes somewhat.

By disaggregating the industrial category into approximately 30 specific industries (listed in table 29), we were able to study the number of industries in which each investment bank plays a significant role. Specifically, for each investment bank we tabulated the number of industries in which the bank's clients account for 10 percent or more of total sales, assets, or income of all *Fortune* 500 companies in their respective industries (see table 17). This part of the analysis provides an important complement to the "number of client relationships" statistics used heretofore. Directly measuring the clients' size and dominance in an industry segment as indicated successively by sales, assets, and income, makes it possible to determine the extent to which reliance on sheer numbers of client relationships distorts the banks' real market penetration and influence.

Not surprisingly, table 17 shows the same group of apex securities firms, those which figured most importantly in the previous breakdowns, on top again. Morgan Stanley, Goldman Sachs, Lehman Brothers, Merrill Lynch, and Salomon Brothers stand out most prominently, accompanied by several other investment banks with a reputation for origination competence. The "number of client relationships" criterion turns out to be a good summary measure of investment banks' overall strength.

The Stability of Client Relationships over Time

Our analysis of the industry's structure to this point has established that a group of leading originating firms dominated the client relationship tables at the end of 1978. But the durability of those liaisons over time has not yet been fully analyzed. Despite the evidence that a consistent group of firms led in underwriting volume at the beginning of the decade and toward the end, it is possible that this observation masks substantial shifting around of client affiliations during the period. Thus, it is important to look at the stability of these bank-client relationships over the period 1970–1978. There are two special reasons for this analysis. First, we suspect that a considerable amount of switching would indicate more vigorous competition.[4] Second, and particularly relevant to our later examination of bank-client matching, it is useful to know to what extent inertia in bank-client relationships may create a persistent state of market disequilibrium in which actual pairings lag behind what might be predicted based on knowledge of the attributes of particular banks and the characteristics and needs of particular clients.

Using *Institutional Investor's* "Who's With Whom" lists for 1973, 1976, and 1978, in table 18 we tabulated total client relationships for our 20-firm sample. The totals were 677 in 1973, 934 in 1976, and 856 in 1978. The increases may be attributable both to the growing use of comanagerships and to the increasing frequency with which third-party securities firms have successfully sold new, special-purpose financing arrangements to corporations already served by other banks. The modest decline between 1976 and 1978 may be attributable to changes in *Institutional Investor's* criteria for defining client relationships.

An analysis of the movement of clients in and out of specific banks also suggests that there was substantial fluidity in bank-client relationships during the 1970s. Table 18 shows that, on a gross basis, the proportion of firms' clients leaving their former bank affiliation was 26 percent between 1973 and 1976 and 30 percent between 1976 and 1978. The proportion of new clients added to the totals of these same firms was 47 percent for 1973–1976 and 23 percent for 1976–1978.

Although differences in these ratios did show up among individual banks, the overall client turnover tended to be quite large for most banks. This is surprising for an industry in which the client relationship had generally been believed to be relatively stable. It is important, therefore, to determine how much the apparent fluidity of client relations actually helped aspiring banks to build greater market share among the most important U.S. corporate clients.

For this investigation, we analyzed the extent to which the special bracket firms—First Boston, Goldman Sachs, Merrill Lynch, Morgan Stanley, and Salomon Brothers—kept large clients among themselves over the period 1970–1978. Here, we utilized a privately compiled list of *Fortune* 500 industrial affiliations in 1970 (Appendix C) and the 1978 *Institutional Investor* list (see table 18).

The results of this analysis are set forth in table 19. The table confirms that there has indeed been a good bit of moving in and out of specific banks' client lists. Most of it, however, has occurred when a former client firm dropped out of the listing universe altogether, that is, failed to use services that would signal a relationship with any investment bank. In fact, almost three-quarters of the client losses of special bracket firms and about two-thirds of the losses of non–special bracket firms were attributable to such "dropouts."

Client bases have been much more stable among the leading originators than among the rest of the sample. During the period studied, only 44 percent of the clients switching from one of the five special bracket firms went to one of the 15 non–special bracket firms, whereas 60 percent of the clients switching from the non–special bracket firms went to a special bracket firm. In the majority of instances, these switching clients either stayed within, or moved into, the special bracket group for new investment banking accommodation.

An analysis of market shares of client relationships reinforces the above conclusion. The last three columns of table 18 give the market shares (measured by number of client relationships) for each of the three selected years. The market-share figures appear to be relatively stable, particularly for the larger banks.

The firm that achieved the greatest market share growth between 1973 and 1978 was Salomon Brothers, which advanced from 2 percent of total client relationships to 7 percent in 1978. This is not an unexpected observation; the growing importance of this particular firm has been widely discussed in trade and other publications. Several firms lost market share between 1970 and 1978. Lehman Brothers, for instance, fell from 17 percent to 10 percent, and Loeb Rhoades from 5 percent to 1 percent.

To recapitulate, results from this part of the study suggest two conclusions: (1) As part of the proliferation in bank relationships during the period 1970–1978, aspiring retail distributors undoubtedly formed relationships with some corporate clients formerly served exclusively by traditionally leading origination firms, particularly through comanagerships and by providing special-purpose financing assistance. (2) Despite the appearance of considerable fluidity in bank-client affiliations, the traditionally leading origination firms have nonetheless maintained a hold on most of their large client bases during the 1970–1978 period.

The analysis in this chapter has confirmed that a relatively small group of investment banks, composed of the five special bracket firms and several others, occupied a dominant position at the beginning of the 1970s and, by and large, sustained that position through 1978, the end of our sample period. This is not to deny that there was some shifting around during this period, or that there was evidence of particular strength or weakness displayed by particular banks in certain client sectors. Nor should it be overlooked that several aspiring retail distribution firms made significant progress during the sample period in their quest for a larger share of the corporate business. This competitive pattern is consistent with the historical evolution of investment banking. Change in the pyramidal structure has taken place only gradually. While there have been new entrants to the apex group, the dislodging of apex firms has been slow, and a number of leading originating firms have sustained their commanding positions over extended periods of time.

This suggests that the barriers to internal mobility noted in the historical development of investment banking continue to operate in the contemporary competitive environment. While Chapter 1 discussed the nature of these barriers in various historical periods, however, it remains to be seen what these impediments are in the contemporary context. It is not yet known what attracts certain types of clients to particular investment banks, nor is there a good statistically based sense of the way in which the industry divides itself into effectively competitive subgroups. Chapters 5 and 6 provide some insights into these questions.

5 The Matching of Banks and Clients

In this chapter we attempt to specify the factors that yield particular bank-client relationships—both factors related to the characteristics of investment banks and those related to the attributes of corporations who are the banks' potential clients. Our hypothesis is that the matching of investment banks to corporate clients results at least in part from differing bank strengths and differing mixes of underwriting skills that corporate clients may value. For example, a corporation that either needs or wants to distribute its new equity shares to individual, noninstitutional investors may seek a bank with a large retail secondary-market brokerage capability. Another firm whose securities sell well to institutional investors may be less interested in retail distribution. The following list shows in its left-hand column several areas in which investment banks can exhibit strengths. Beside each of these items we indicate several measurable variables that may partially index those strengths.

Investment banks will excel to varying degrees in each of these areas, and clients presumably evaluate investment banks on all these dimensions. Over time, then, a corporation presumably moves to the investment bank or banks whose major strengths best match the corporation's needs.

Strength	Index of Strength
Expertise in corporate finance	Mergers and acquisitions business Number of corporate finance professionals Clients per corporate finance professional Size of clients Share of various markets and submarkets
Retail distribution capability	Number of retail registered representatives
Institutional distribution capability	Number of institutional registered representatives
Expertise in client's industry	Share of clients (or assets) within industry Industry research score
Research capability	Industry research score Overall research score
International corporate finance and distribution capability	Number of international corporate professionals and brokerage executives

The Logit Model

To analyze the determinants of client-bank relationships we have employed a statistical technique known as logit analysis. The logit model is one way of translating these general ideas about the matching of banks and clients into a statistical model. It provides a framework within which to assess the relative importance to specific clients of specific bank strengths. For example, we can study not only whether expertise about the client's industry affects a client's choices, but also how much it affects them relative to other possible bank strengths. Using logit analysis, we will test various hypotheses about what factors influence choices.

The logit model combines the characteristics of the sellers and buyers in a market to generate a probability that a particular seller and buyer with certain characteristics will be matched. To the extent that the choice-causing attributes of investment banks and clients are measurable, it is possible to capture those determinants of choice in a model designed to explain the probability that they will be matched. In other words, the model is designed to summarize how measurable differences in investment banks and their corporate clients interact to affect the choices of banks by clients.[1] To the degree that the model is successful (that is, that it accurately describes choices), it will tell us something about the characteristics of investment banks that attract particular types of clients.

Thus, it provides a way for us to assess the extent to which particular investment banks may have proprietary holds on those parts of the market they occupy; conversely, it yields insights about the extent to which banks with dissimilar characteristics are likely to be able to attract each others' clients.

The logit analysis, however, does not deal with at least one important aspect of competition: the ease or difficulty with which an investment bank can adjust its own characteristics. The choice model thus provides no direct evidence on the presence or absence of barriers to intergroup mobility.[2]

Hypotheses and Variables in the Model

The summary data discussed in Chapter 4 strongly suggested that the client bases of the major investment banks differ in important dimensions. This observation leads to the general hypothesis that the market for corporate underwriting services is segmented at least to some degree. According to this hypothesis, investment banks have different strengths, and the relative importance of these strengths differs from one corporate client to the next. Therefore, the pairing of banks with corporate clients should in principle be related to characteristics of both banks and clients.

The probability that a corporation will choose a particular investment bank as its principal bank depends upon the characteristics and needs of that corporation and upon the characteristics of all the investment banks from which it can choose. The data for estimating the determinants of these probabilities are the characteristics of banks and clients and the choices that corporate clients have actually made.

Prospective clients will evaluate banks' strengths in various areas, several of which were listed at the beginning of this chapter. We now disuss these strengths and the problem of how to measure them quantitatively for use in a statistical analysis.

Expertise in corporate finance is probably the most important strength that clients examine in evaluating investment banks. While we cannot measure expertise directly, we can use several indices of expertise. One index is the size of the corporate finance staff; larger staffs may have greater expertise generally or in specific areas. Various characteristics of banks' existing client bases provide additional indices of corporate finance strength. For example, a bank's share of clients in a specific industry may signal to other prospective clients in that industry the bank's ability to meet their needs. A bank's client base may also indicate the extent to which it can draw upon a network of contacts that could be useful in the context of a merger and acquisition assignment. Finally, the bank's client base may include prestige clients (as measured, perhaps, by size or bond rating), which may in turn signal substantial market respect for that bank and thus the prospect of good reception for other securities carrying the bank's imprimatur. In short, the quality of a bank's corporate finance staff—measured by its size, by the characteristics of its client base, and by other indices—is likely to influence clients' choices of investment banks.

An investment bank may also have other strengths that appeal to corporate clients. One such strength is the ability to distribute securities to both institutional and retail customers. Another is a bank's presence in international or foreign securities markets at both the corporate finance and distribution levels. Similarly, a bank may have developed special expertise in particular industries or particular kinds of securities. Industry expertise may derive not only from experience with other clients in the same or related industries, a source of expertise already discussed, but also from the work of the bank's securities analysts.

Because clients differ, they will value these attributes differently. Most obviously, they operate in different industries and therefore value expertise in specific industries differently. Similarly, a client's securities may appeal particularly to either individual or institutional investors, and the client will logically value a bank's particular distribution capabilities accordingly.

These examples suggest the general approach of the analysis. With the selection of variables in the model, the hypotheses will become more precise.

Twenty-five variables were selected that might be likely to influence the matching process, ranging from measures of corporate finance capability and research competence to measures of securities distribution capacity. The variables are listed in the left hand column of tables 20 and 21. (A detailed discussion of these variables is presented in Appendix B.) Where characteristics likely to influence bank-client matching were not directly observable, the best proxies available were used. For example, a bank's expertise regarding a particular industry was measured in part by whether its analysts for that particular industry had been selected for inclusion on *Institutional Investor*'s All-American Research Team. The other measure for industry expertise is the bank's market share in the potential client's industry.

As in Chapter 4, we carried out our analysis using both the *Institutional Investor* and the lead manager criteria. Since the nature of the relationship is different under the two tests, differences were expected and found in the attributes of banks and clients that affect the probabilities of a match (despite the general congruence of results under the two sets of criteria noted in Chapter 4).

For purposes of summary, each of the 25 independent variables used in the logit model can be identified with one of five categories of bank attributes: size and quality of the corporate finance department; expertise in particular types of offerings; expertise in the international area; expertise in and dominance of a client's particular industry; and distribution capacity. Tables 20 and 21 report the results of the logit analysis. Here we explain the major hypotheses and summarize the statistical results obtained in the logit analysis (for more detail see Appendix B).

Corporate finance department size, quality, prestige, and experience. The hypothesis was that all clients, other things being equal, would be attracted to the more prestigious, experienced, and skilled investment banking firms. The statistical results suggest that the presence of large companies among the clients of an investment bank does seem to attract other large corporate clients but not smaller clients, although this may reflect selectivity on the part of the investment bank.

Another independent variable used to measure corporate finance capability was the number of corporate finance professionals at each investment bank. The hypothesis was that banks with larger staffs would attract more clients. The statistical results confirm a correlation, although it is not clear in which direction causality runs. It could be that banks with more clients hire more corporate finance professionals. If the latter is true, the statistical results cannot be interpreted to show that bolstering one's corporate finance staff attracts clients.

In general, however, the statistical analysis suggests that the more prestigious, experienced, and skilled an investment bank, the more likely it is to attract clients. The number of clients per corporate finance professional picks this up in the logit equations.

Expertise in particular types of offerings. The hypothesis was that corporate clients with a particular interest in issuing debt or equity, or which often use competitive bidding, would be attracted to investment banks with particular expertise in these types of offerings. The results show that utilities are indeed attracted to investment banks with a leading position in competitive bid underwritings, even though the selection of the lead managers for each successive competitive underwriting is handled by sealed bid. Contrary to the hypothesis, however, we found that fast-growing firms that rely heavily on debt financing do not gravitate toward the securities firms with leading positions in underwriting debt securities. Perhaps those securities firms are wary of the relatively high levels of financial risk implicit in the capital structures of these corporate issuers and do not readily accept their business.

Expertise or presence in the international area. We expected that investment banks with large international corporate finance staffs and international securities sales forces would attract clients with substantial international business (as measured by the proportion of their total sales accounted for by sales abroad). However, the findings do not provide statistical support for such a relationship.

Expertise in and dominance of a client's particular industry. Most large American investment banks serving the major American national corporate issuers maintain research staffs that study a wide range of industries for the benefit of customers to whom they provide investment advisory services. The hypothesis was first that banks with overall research strength would attract clients. In addition, it was hypothesized that possessing research strength in a particular industry might help attract underwriting clients from that industry.

Our findings indicate that general research competence does

not attract underwriting clients. We do find, however, that clients are attracted to investment banks that have a particularly strong research capability in their specific industry or that already have clients in their industry. In several industries, a few banks hold a high percentage of the client population.

Distribution capacity. We hypothesized that investment banks with substantial in-house distribution capacity—both institutional and retail—would have an advantage in attracting clients. The statistical results, however, support the hypothesis only with respect to institutional, not retail, distribution capacity. While firms with more *institutional* registered representatives do, as expected, attract more underwriting clients, firms with more *retail* capacity are less likely to attract clients. This anomalous finding about the effect of retail capacity may be attributable to any of several factors. One possibility is that retail orientation is negatively correlated with corporate finance quality. Alternatively, there may be a disequilibrium in which the growth of some banks' corporate finance staffs has lagged behind a recent, rapid growth of the firms' retail brokerage capacity.

Several other tests of the effect of distribution capacity also yielded surprising results. For example, we found that having a large institutional brokerage staff does not necessarily attract clients a substantial portion of whose securities are held by institutions. One explanation of this finding is that client issuers look primarily at investment banks' corporate finance skills, and assume that distribution to institutions can be carried out by firms other than the client's principal investment bank.

For each investment bank, the model described above estimates 750 individual probability figures. Each one is the probability that the bank will have one of the 750 corporations as a client. These probabilities vary according to the likelihood that the bank will successfully attract a particular corporation as a client. Each bank's predicted total market share is, then, the proportion of the total number of clients for which the estimated probability of choosing that bank is greater than the estimated probability of choosing any other bank. Table 22 gives predicted and actual shares for the tenth specification under the lead manager criterion.[3] The model yields predicted market shares that are very close to actual market shares.

* * *

In this chapter we studied the determinants of the probability that a particular client will match with a particular investment bank. Using logit analysis, we identified a number of specific, observable variables that affect these probabilities, and other variables that do not. Then, given the actual characteristics of the banks and corporations in our sample, we computed the share of clients that the model predicts each bank would have. In the next chapter we use the same model, and the probability figures it generated, to study similarities and differences between investment banks. In this way, we can show that the investment banking industry is composed of several groups, each containing a few banks, and that banks in the same group compete more directly for clients than do banks in different groups.

6 Competitive Groups in the Industry

In approaching the task of identifying meaningful subgroups of contemporary investment banking competitors, we might begin by thinking of each corporation as a market. Each investment bank has some probability of attracting that corporation as a client. The probabilities across banks can be thought of as market shares, much as the average probability across all clients is close to actual share if the model is accurate. If we interpret each separate corporation as a market, we can calculate the drawing power of the leading competitors for the business of each corporation in terms of probabilities. For each corporation we calculate the sum, c_{jk}, of the largest k probabilities among the $\hat{P}_{ij}$, $i = 1, \ldots, 20$ for $k = 1, \ldots, 5$. These numbers are measures of the concentration of probability for each separate corporation. There are more than 700 corporations in the sample. Several different specifications, that is, combinations of influential factors, were tried. When the more rigorous lead managership criterion was used, the predicted probabilities did not differ dramatically from specification to specification. Therefore we have selected one representative specification and present its statistical results in table 23.

Table 24 shows the average values of $c_{j1}, \ldots, c_{j5}$ over all corporations in the sample. It also reports the standard deviations for each. Averaged across all corporations, the top bank with the highest probability has a 17 percent chance of attracting the corporation as a client. (The bank with the highest probability, of course, varies from corporation to corporation.) The second-ranking bank has roughly a 14 percent chance, the third about 11 percent, the fourth about 9 percent, and the fifth about 8 percent. These submarkets are (according to the model) highly concentrated, and somewhat more so than the overall market (see table 21 for actual market shares and table 24 for the overall concentration data).

Table 24 also gives the average Herfindahl index (H) across corporations. The Herfindahl index is another measure of concentration. It has the value 1 if there is a monopoly, and $1/n$ if the market has n firms with equal shares. Its inverse is sometimes interpreted as the hypothetical number of firms in the industry. For corporation j, the Herfindahl index would be the sum of the squares of the predicted probabilities

$$H_j = \Sigma_i \hat{P}_{ij}^2$$

and the average Herfindahl index across corporations is

$$H = \sum_{j=1}^{J} H_j/J.$$

Thus, table 24 suggests that the actual industry population of 18 investment banking firms of varying strengths would be the equivalent of a hypothetical investment banking industry composed of 11 firms of identical size and strength.

Competitive Groups

The purpose of this analysis of the matching of banks and clients is to help us understand the intraindustry competitive structure of the market. One way to gain understanding might be to use the measured attributes of banks to see which banks appear to have similar attributes. It is very likely true that banks that compete closely for a particular group of clients will have similar measured attributes. But if we were to proceed in this fashion we would not know which attributes (or combinations of attributes) were particularly important. Nor would this approach factor in the preferences of potential clients except to the extent that some of a bank's measured attributes are average characteristics of its client base.

Thus we took a different approach, one that uses the logit model, to assess the competitive structure of the market. We should emphasize that the competitive group analysis below is to be regarded not as a "test" of the model, but rather as an exploration of the model's implications, on the assumption that the model itself is a reasonable approximation to reality.

For each investment bank, there are $J = 750$ predicted probabilities $\hat{p}_{i1}$. The vector of probabilities $(\hat{p}_{i1}, \ldots, \hat{p}_{ij})$ is symbolized by P_i. To assess who competes with whom, we consider the correlation coefficients between pairs of vectors P_i and P_k. If the correlation coefficient for P_i and P_k, $\rho(P_i,P_k)$, is positive and near one, then the two banks compete for the same clients in the sense that relative to overall market share, their probabilities of attracting a particular corporation tend to be high or low together. Table 25 gives all the correlation coefficients for pairs of investment banks in the sample.[1] Banks with relatively high correlation coefficients have been grouped together. A competitive group is now defined to be a collection of banks such that $\rho(P_i,P_k)$ is greater than 0.5 for any pair within the group and $\rho(P_i,P_k)$ is less than 0.5 for a pair with one in the group and one out. It is clear that with this definition there might be no competitive groups.[2]

In fact, by this definition there are four nearly perfect competitive groups. They are easily visible in table 25. The correlation coefficients in the diagonal blocks are all positive and greater than 0.5 (generally well above 0.8). The correlation coefficients in the off-diagonal blocks are almost all below 0.5, and they are generally large in absolute value and negative. Thus not only are there competitive groups but they appear to be quite distinct in their drawing power with respect to segments of the client base. The banks in each group are as follows:

Group I	Bache	Group III	Dillon, Read
	Bear, Stearns		Drexel Burnham
	E. F. Hutton		Goldman Sachs
	First Boston		Lehman Brothers
	Kidder, Peabody		Morgan Stanley
	Loeb Rhoades		Warburg
	Paine, Webber		
	Smith Barney		
Group II	Merrill Lynch	Group IV	Blyth Eastman
	Salomon Brothers		Dean Witter

There are only two imperfections in this grouping relative to the standard defined above; both concern Group IV. As can be seen from table 25, Blyth Eastman and Dean Witter have correlation coefficients greater than 0.5 with some but not all of the firms in Group III. They could have been included in Group III, but it seemed more informative to separate them. Blyth Eastman has a correlation below 0.5 with Dillon Read, Goldman Sachs, and Morgan Stanley. Dean Witter has a low correlation with Goldman Sachs and Morgan Stanley.

Before we proceed, it is important to review the rationale for the approach to competitive grouping that we have adopted here. There are in the data empirical distributions of the attributes of banks and clients. We use these distributions to carry out a type of cluster analysis for banks that is competitively relevant. In cluster analysis, each bank is associated with a vector of attributes, and then the distance between banks is measured. The vector of attributes used here is P_i, the vector of predicted probabilities for bank i that emerge from the logit model. The predicted probabilities are measures of the banks' drawing power in each of 750 markets defined to be the markets for the underwriting work of each of those 750 corporations. Since these predicted probabilities are summary statistics calculated from the distributions of bank and client characteristics and of actual choices, and are designed to "predict" choices, they appear to meet the standard of competitive relevance as attributes of banks. They are summaries of competitive strength in all the submarkets.

One way to think of the logit regression is as an attempt to measure competitive strength from data on attributes and choices. More precisely, it estimates the parameters in a function (the choice probability function) whose purpose is to determine competitive strength in each submarket.

Cluster analysis itself can be simple or very complicated at the discretion of the analyst. Because it seems to yield interesting insights in this case, we employ one of the simpler approaches, using pairwise correlations to measure distance between competitors. Our use of this approach is not meant to imply that more sophisticated cluster analysis techniques would not be useful. But cluster analysis can involve a highly complicated set of technical problems that would go beyond the scope of this book.

It is of some interest to compare the groups that emerge from the logit model with the groupings commonly used in the securities industry. The relationship is shown in table 26.

Group I is dominated by national wirehouse (retail brokerage) firms. Two originating firms—First Boston and Kidder Peabody—are included in this group. Given Kidder's strong historical distribution capability, its membership in this group is understandable. The inclusion of First Boston is puzzling, since it has no significant retail distribution and, as we saw in the profile analysis, it shares origination leadership with only a handful of other industry firms.

All but two of the Group III firms are classified by the industry as large investment banks and are noteworthy for their leadership in origination. And at least one of the two retail brokerage firms in Group III (Drexel Burnham) has an antecedent firm with a historical position in investment banking. Both Drexel Burnham and Warburg have relatively small client bases, and a significant proportion of these banks' capital comes from Europe.

The Group II firms—Merrill Lynch and Salomon Brothers—are now considered special bracket banking firms. But their original strength was in distribution: retail brokerage in the case of Merrill Lynch and institutional brokerage in the case of Salomon Brothers.

Group IV has one industry-designated large investment bank (Blyth Eastman) and one industry-designated national wirehouse firm (Dean Witter). In reality, however, these two firms appear to occupy similar market niches. Both are substantial retail distributors, and each has a predecessor firm component that originated on the West Coast. At the end of the sample period both firms continued to enjoy a strong competitive position in the Far West.

Thus, while the groupings based on the model are not identical to the groupings acknowledged by the securities industry itself, they are closely related. This similarity suggests that while a number of firms historically associated with securities distribution have made efforts to diversify and to expand their operations into underwriting–corporate finance, at the end of the sample period in 1978 their success varied widely. Group I firms (with the exception of First Boston and Kidder Peabody) continued to draw their principal strength from their distribution capabilities. By the beginning of the 1970s, the two Group II firms had already successfully moved from largely distribution activities to a mix of activities that included leading positions in investment banking. Still, they remained somewhat different from the origination firms (Group III) in their competitive strengths. The two firms in Group IV have the characteristics of origination firms, but seem to lack to some extent the capacity to compete head-to-head with the origination leaders in Group III, Morgan Stanley, Goldman Sachs, and Lehman Brothers.

An obvious question is, how different are these four groups? There are several possible ways to answer this question. One is to look at the correlations between pairs drawn from different groups. A rough assessment of the results of that exercise is presented in table 27 and figure 15.[3] Groups I and III, the two largest, are really quite different. Typically, the correlation between any pair of investment firms, one from each of these two groups, is about −0.7. An observer could probably cite numerous examples of vigorous competition for a particular client's business between firms in these two groups. Nonetheless, our statistical tests suggest that over a broad spectrum of client possibilities the market divides roughly into two segments, with the securities firms in a group competing among themselves for potential clients much more than they compete with the firms in the other group.

The two remaining groups are in some sense in the middle. Group II is modestly negatively correlated with Group I and more strongly negatively correlated with Group III. That is, on average, Merrill Lynch and Salomon Brothers are more likely to compete for the clients of the securities firms in Group I (most of which have large retail distribution capabilities) than for those of the origination leaders in Group III.

The firms in Group IV (Blyth Eastman and Dean Witter) are very close in market segment to the competitors in Group III. They are, however, only modestly negatively correlated with Groups I and II, and therefore may on occasion find themselves competing in these markets as well.

For completeness, table 28 provides predicted and actual shares for the four groups. As with individual banks, the predicted shares are close to actual shares.

Group Profiles

We now return to our data on the characteristics of banks and their clients. This time the data are organized by competitive

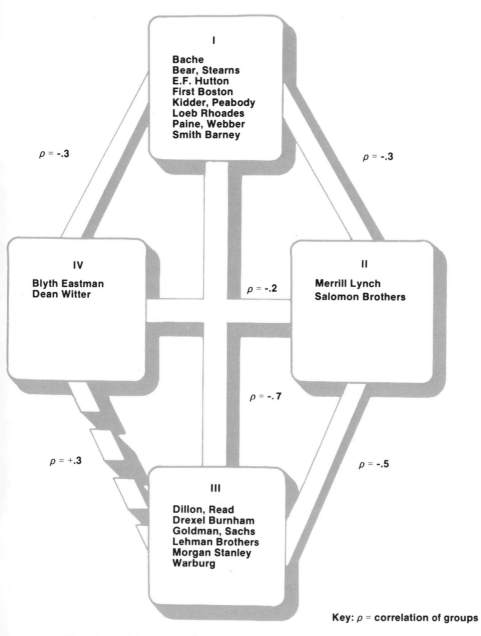

I

Bache
Bear, Stearns
E.F. Hutton
First Boston
Kidder, Peabody
Loeb Rhoades
Paine, Webber
Smith Barney

ρ = -.3

ρ = -.3

IV

Blyth Eastman
Dean Witter

ρ = -.2

II

Merrill Lynch
Salomon Brothers

ρ = -.7

ρ = +.3

ρ = -.5

III

Dillon, Read
Drexel Burnham
Goldman, Sachs
Lehman Brothers
Morgan Stanley
Warburg

Key: ρ = correlation of groups

15 The relationships among the
competitive groups

group rather than by bank. Tables 29 and 30 present the group shares of client relationships in 33 industries. Tables 31 and 32 show group shares of these industries on the basis of industry assets. For example, table 31 shows Group I with a 24 percent share of the mining and oil exploration industry. This means that clients of Group I banks owned approximately 24 percent of the total assets of firms in this industry. Table 33 summarizes the average characteristics of the banks and their clients for each group.

Group I does not have a major presence in many industrials; this is somewhat surprising when one considers the large number of banks in this group. This group is stronger in retailing, transportation, and utilities. The clients of Group I banks tend to be smaller (measured by average sales, assets, income, and equity) than those of other groups. Its clients also have the lowest average bond rating, the lowest percentage of their stock institutionally held, and the lowest percentage of their sales made outside the United States. Interestingly, Group I banks have a lower percentage of their total registered representatives working in the institutional and foreign areas than do those of any other group. The average Group I bank also has fewer corporate finance professionals than the average bank of any of the other three groups.

Though it has a major share of only a few industrials (mining, publishing, and motor vehicles), Group II's share of the major industrial sectors is quite impressive when one considers that the group comprises only two firms (Merrill Lynch and Salomon Brothers). This group also has very large market shares among commercial banks, diversified financial companies, transportation companies, and utilities. The Group II banks employ, by a large margin, the most registered representatives in all three categories (domestic retail, institutional, and foreign), as well as the most corporate finance professionals, reflecting in substantial part the presence of giant Merrill Lynch as one of the two firms in that group. These banks handled a high volume of mergers and received the highest average research score. Though their clients rank first among the groups in average sales growth and have high average assets, Group II's clients generally rank third in the other characteristics included in table 33. Group II's clients have a significantly lower return on assets than clients of the other groups, possibly reflecting the presence of many financial institutions in its client base.

Group III possesses the largest market share in most of the industrial categories and, because of the inclusion of Goldman Sachs, in retailing. Group III has shares comparable to those of Group II in commercial banking, diversified financial, transportation, and utilities categories, but includes four more investment banks than Group II. Group III banks have far fewer total sales representatives, and a smaller average capital base. Considering their size, Group III firms employ a very large number of corporate finance professionals. These banks also average, by a large margin, the highest merger volume. Group III's clients have the highest average sales and relatively high net income. Clients of the Group III firms also have the highest percentage of their stock held by institutions and the greatest percentage of their sales made abroad.

Group IV includes only two banks—Blyth Eastman and Dean Witter. This group has large market shares in only a few industries (computers, ships and railways, and, based on comanagerships, mining and oil exploration). The Group IV banks average the second-highest number of registered representatives, with a very high percentage of them devoted to domestic retail. Their ratio of corporate finance professionals to registered representatives is the lowest among the groups. These two banks handle a small volume of mergers, and have the lowest research score. It may be somewhat misleading to compare the averages of Group IV's clients to those of other groups, however, because the Group IV banks serve relatively few clients (thus increasing the potential effect on the averages of a few very large clients). But we should note that Group IV's clients had the highest average assets and net income and sold at a significantly lower price/earnings ratio. Furthermore, Group IV's clients averaged the highest equity and produced a substantially higher return on equity than did the other groups' clients.

The model employed here surely captures only part of the internal structure relevant to competition in investment banking. Specialized areas of expertise that banks may possess are sometimes hard to measure, but only if measured can they be analyzed statistically. With richer data, it might be possible to divide firms more finely into competitive groups and subgroups.

Despite the limitations of the data, we were able to discern four competitive groups. While firms in different groups certainly do compete with one another, firms compete more frequently with other firms in the same group. In fact, the correlation coefficient between the two largest groups (I and III) is negative 0.7.

These logit-identified competitive groups are similar to industry-acknowledged categories, although they are certainly not identical. The groups' respective client bases have noticeably different characteristics.

The data do not suggest an absence of competition. For individual corporate clients, concentration based on the predicted probabilities from the model is high, but not substantially different from the concentration in the market as a whole. Thus, while the market is quite far from being homogeneous, it does not give the appearance of being so segmented that there are very few firms competing for any given corporation's business.

From the standpoint of competitive stability, an important question is whether Group II firms with their combination of assets and corporate relationships will acquire client-attracting capacities over time that will be difficult for competing securities firms to counter. The evidence presented here suggests, however, that the client bases and competitive strengths of Groups I and III are quite different. Further, while the Group II firms lie somewhere between the two traditional groups, there is no strong evidence to suggest that this position gives these two firms a special advantage in acquiring additional market shares in either client base. If, for example, the dummy variables for Merrill Lynch or Salomon Brothers in the logit analysis had turned up with positive and significant coefficients, then we might suspect that the hybrid was in some sense more than the sum of its parts. But the investigation revealed no such result.

If this judgment is approximately correct, then it is not surprising that the traditional apex investment banks have not felt great pressure to diversify into retail distribution and related activities. The brokerage firms may continue their efforts to diversify into corporate finance and underwriting, because these are profitable activities. But the process of building a corporate finance capability and reputation is very time consuming. As the long history of investment banking has shown, such changes in the pyramidal structure come only slowly. Hence, there do not seem to be intraindustry forces that in the near term would cause dramatic shifts in competitive structure. But such forces could arise from other quarters, and we will discuss them briefly in the concluding chapter.

Conclusion

In our exploration of competition within the underwriting–corporate finance sector of the securities industry, we have sought not only to encompass the traditional study of industry concentration trends but also to investigate the underlying competitive structure that produces the pattern of concentration.

The historical review described a line of business with considerable stability over an extended period of time. It suggested that investment banking has long tended to assume a pyramidal competitive structure, with a few preeminent firms providing leadership in both financing and collateral services. This structure was probably reinforced by the Glass-Steagall Act, which barred entry by banks—a group of well-positioned potential entrants.

The U.S. economic expansion of the late 1950s and 1960s created favorable conditions for advancement by several ambitious firms at the secondary levels of the pyramid; by the early 1970s three of them, Goldman Sachs, Merrill Lynch, and Salomon Brothers had advanced to positions among the apex group, supplanting several other firms of declining fortunes.

Our more detailed statistical study of the 1970s did not reveal any fundamental breach with the historical pattern. There was no dramatic fragmentation of the business, no substantial flattening out of the pyramid. In fact, examination of underwriting volume data for that period suggests that there was actually a tendency toward increased concentration in investment banking. When gross underwriting revenue is substituted for dollar volume of managed underwritings, a similar trend toward increased concentration is noted. An inverse period-to-period link between concentration and combined negotiated and competitive financing activity also was observed. It appears that during slack periods managing underwriters both obtain a larger share of the available underwriting business and keep larger shares of the revenue pie for themselves and their distribution systems, at least in the case of equity financings. While we recognize that the revenue data are less precise than the dollar volume data (because in the revenue data negotiated and competitive offering figures are lumped together), we are convinced that revenue share figures provide a complementary insight to the results of the dollar volume analysis.

Some observers of the industry maintain, however, that concentration analysis masks a competitive structure more complex than that suggested by aggregate concentration data. The historical record of investment banking and our analysis of characteristics of investment banks and their clients in the late 1970s support that contention. The results of the logit analysis suggest that there are indeed distinct market segments within which substantial competition takes place but between which competition may be much less robust. The groupings derived by the logit analysis are similar but far from identical to the categories established by the Securities Industry Association. They are also congruent with the hierarchy reflected in the underwriting syndicate structure used by the securities industry. This is not to suggest that the groupings derived here completely describe or explain competition in investment banking. Indeed, when our results are compared with field observations, several firms seem mistyped. Field observations also suggest that the model may understate the amount of competition between groups. Moreover, some newer entrants into the industry were not included in the study.

Nonetheless, while the model does not provide a completely faithful description of contemporary competitive patterns, it seems clearly to point in the right direction. Recognition that there are, in fact, distinct market segments is an important first step toward more meaningful analysis of competition in investment banking and toward subsequent framing of appropriate public policy guidelines.

This study suggests that certain types of clients and industries tend to gravitate toward investment banks with certain profiles.

Larger and higher-quality corporate clients tend to affiliate with the industry-acknowledged underwriting leaders. Moreover, those prized clients tend to remain with leading banks, even while using the services of other banks for specific transactions. The data suggest that there may indeed be barriers to client mobility among the market segments, but the impediment is probably asymmetrical. A special bracket bank is more likely to attract a client away from a distribution firm than is a distribution firm to attract a client from a special bracket bank. The distribution firms, despite their impressive commitment of resources to corporate finance over an extended period of time, have had great difficulty in increasing their share of the prime clients traditionally served by the apex firms.

The investment banking industry evolved gradually, and our analysis of concentration trends and of bank-client relationships might lead one to expect similarly gradual change in the future. The predictive value of such extrapolation, however, is by no means certain. Indeed, our final question—one we will answer only with impressions, not with statistical analysis—is whether the continuity observed in the recent past is likely to characterize the future. Or, instead, will changes in banks and clients—and in the financial and regulatory framework within which they operate—dramatically reshape the investment banking industry.

In addressing this question, it is important to distinguish several segments of the securities industry. Many important recent developments have occurred in the retail brokerage business: for example, the acquisition of Dean Witter by Sears, of Bache by Prudential Insurance, and of Shearson by American Express. While the past decade has also seen some important mergers and some impressive innovations in product line and strategic direction by both the apex investment banks and those lower in the pyramidal hierarchy, the traditional industry structure has remained largely intact. Our historical review identified several key ingredients for success in this business: an environment that is entrepreneurial, the capacity for fast response, and the capability of attracting and holding talented individuals. Historically, the organizational structure that has best accommodated this has been a relatively small, free-form institution similar to one of the leading apex firms, rather than a large, multilayered bureaucratic structure similar to a commercial bank or a financial services conglomerate.

Undoubtedly, there will be major changes in the way financial intermediaries pursue the available underwriting–corporate finance business in the future. In fact, in 1982 trade publications such as *Institutional Investor* were chronicling the almost cutthroat tactics being employed by a number of U.S. securities firms in the quest for new business.

It seems likely that as time goes on the trend toward increasing in-house competence in corporate finance among U.S. business firms will continue. This may contribute to acceleration in the rate at which financial products mature from innovations, at the time of their introduction, to commodity-like services supplied in more or less the same form by a variety of intermediaries. Thus, the half-life of new, innovative financing ideas may grow shorter as they are quickly copied by investment banking competitors and, ultimately, by the in-house staffs of issuers themselves. Although the investment banking leaders have historically shown the ability to adapt relatively quickly to such change, we can only speculate about their nimbleness in the years ahead.

The possible repercussions of substantial modification or replacement of the Glass-Steagall Act must also be considered in any speculation about industry structure in the future. Our historical sketch indicates that the structure of the investment banking industry is the product of many influences, only one of which— albeit an important one—is the regulatory framework. Thus, removal of the entry barriers established by Glass-Steagall would not necessarily precipitate a massive, near-term restructuring of the industry.

One important factor reinforcing the pyramidal structure of investment banking over time has been the requirements of the underwriting process itself. To be sure, there are important changes taking place in the underwriting function within the securities markets, including a regulatory relaxation via SEC Rule 415, which has the effect of permitting certain frequent corporate issuers to maintain a continuous, updated registration statement with the SEC so that underwritings can be launched with very little advance preparation or lost time.

We anticipate that this will lead some issuers to seek bids from one or a small group of very well capitalized securities firms rather than rely upon the traditional, broad-based syndicate organization. Such a move would be likely to give a special advantage to securities firms with substantial in-house distribution capacity and the capital to inventory securities temporarily while seeking investor outlets. This practice would find a historical analog in the practice followed by the special-bracket securities firms before the 1930s; they would buy blocks of securities from corporate or government issuers and then subcontract their sale to ultimate investors through other, distribution-oriented securities firms. It is unclear whether the principal effect of this development will be to alter fundamentally the outline of the pyramidal structure or to provide a means by which some firms propel themselves into more prominent positions within the pyramid at the expense of some of the incumbent leaders.

The increasing integration of the U.S. capital markets with other capital markets around the world raises other issues that we have not directly studied here. What would be the impact on the U.S. investment banking business of a shift toward integrated global capital markets, with individual national markets and the rapidly growing supranational Euromarket linked together electronically? In fact, the U.S. investment banks have been moving aggressively to position themselves to survive—and thrive—within such a world market. The firms are now firmly committed both to servicing their U.S. corporate client bases abroad and to soliciting the business of other foreign capital users and investors. Their syndicate, pricing, and market-making skills have helped them to establish strong positions in these markets. Moreover, the perception of the U.S. as a last safe haven for flight capital from around the world has given them, along with U.S. commercial banks, a special advantage in soliciting foreign business.

The prospect of an influx of foreign merchant banks, or universal banks with merchant banking competence, into the U.S. market also has to be considered. There would appear to be opportunities for such foreign intermediaries to make convincing appeals to some U.S. corporations and investors with broad geographical interests. However, it is unclear to what extent these foreign banks could outflank the leading U.S. investment banks, which have a long history of innovation and competitive vigor.

Thus, we conclude that these new factors in the investment banking industry, while potentially weighty in their impact, do not necessarily foreshadow a dramatic departure from the competitive pattern we have chronicled.

A Analysis of Corporate Relationships

Industry Concentration: *Institutional Investor* Criterion

Using *Institutional Investor's* "Who's With Whom" list for 1978, we tabulated the securities firms' representation among clients in *Fortune's* six major industry categories. The results, which are presented in table 14 and discussed briefly in Chapter 4, are treated in more detail here.

Generally, those firms which had 6 percent or more of the corporate relationships constitute essentially the same group that had historically led in underwriting volume (with the exclusion of three firms in the category of large investment banks—Dillon Read, Lazard Frères, and Smith Barney). The firms with the largest shares of the total corporate relationships were as follows:

Goldman, Sachs	14.8%	Morgan Stanley	8.2%
Merrill Lynch	14.3%	Salomon Brothers	7.0%
Lehman Brothers	9.8%	Blyth Eastman	6.0%
First Boston	9.1%		

A similar pattern appears if we look only at the industrial clients (the firms in the *Fortune* 500). The following firms had the largest shares of industrial corporate relationships:

Goldman, Sachs	17.7%	First Boston	8.3%
Merrill Lynch	12.6%	Kidder, Peabody	6.6%
Lehman Brothers	10.7%	Blyth Eastman	6.3%
Morgan Stanley	8.9%		

Salomon Brothers, with past strengths focusing on nonindustrial categories such as financial and transportation company issues, has a relatively low (4.1 percent) share of industrial clients; Lazard Frères and Smith Barney are just below the 6 percent share cutoff.

Table 16 indicates that roughly 50 percent of the client relationships were held by the top four firms and 75 percent by the top eight firms at the end of 1978.

That certain investment houses occupy special niches in the industry is pointed up, for instance, in the commercial banking sector; three firms have particularly important shares of commercial bank relationships:

Merrill Lynch	19.4%
First Boston	14.9%
Salomon Brothers	13.4%

Below this group, Dean Witter, Goldman Sachs, and Lehman Brothers each have 9 percent of the bank relationships. Table 16 shows that at the end of 1978 approximately 57 percent of the relationships with commercial banks were concentrated in the top four firms and 87 percent in the top eight firms.

Among diversified financial firms such as finance companies, insurance companies, and savings and loan stock companies, several of the same securities firms were leaders:

Salomon Brothers	21.2%
Blyth Eastman	15.2%
First Boston	9.1%
Merrill Lynch	9.1%

That three of these four firms are also the leading intermediaries for commercial banks suggests that special competences attached to certain investment banks may help in securing client relationships within finance-oriented industries. Salomon Brothers' origin as a small house specializing in the securities of commercial banks probably contributed to establishing its current leading position with both bank and diversified financial issuers.

That an investment bank's historical origins influence its client base is confirmed in examining the shares of relationships with retailing companies:

Goldman, Sachs	26.8%
Lehman Brothers	19.6%
Merrill Lynch	19.6%

Goldman Sachs traces its origins back to itinerant peddlers in the mid-nineteenth century, while Lehman Brothers had its start as cotton brokers and retailers in the South during the same period. Table 16 shows that the top four firms control an inordinately large 71 percent of the retailing relationships; the top eight have 86 percent.

In the transportation sector, at least one leading firm, Lehman Brothers, also has a special historical relationship with the industry by virtue of predecessor firm Kuhn Loeb's close identification with the growth of the U.S. railroads. Historically this relationship was vividly illustrated by the clash between Kuhn Loeb and J. P. Morgan for control of the Union Pacific at the turn of the century. The following firms have the leading shares of transportation company relationships:

Salomon Brothers	23.9%
Bache	10.9%
Lehman Brothers	10.9%
First Boston	8.7%
Goldman, Sachs	8.7%

Public utilities need large and continuing supplies of outside funds; they especially emphasize a banking firm's ability to place securities. A particular premium attaches to retail placement capability (either in-house or through syndicate leadership), since institutional absorption capacity is limited, particularly for utilities with lower credit ratings. Three firms have the largest market shares of utilities company relationships:

Merrill Lynch	21.4%
First Boston	12.5%
Morgan Stanley	11.6%

Significantly, several other firms with substantial retail capability also have respectable market shares: Kidder Peabody (8.0 percent), Dean Witter (7.1 percent), E. F. Hutton (6.3 percent), and Bache (5.4 percent). Table 16 shows that concentration of relationships in the utility area is not inordinate, with about 53 percent in the hands of the top four firms and 80 percent in the hands of the top eight firms. The utility issuers are obviously casting a wide net in their search for intermediary relationships that will yield the necessary financing results.

Industry Concentration: Lead Manager Criterion

When we look at the distribution of client relationships using the lead manager criterion between 1973 and 1978 (refer to table 15) a pattern similar to that provided by the *Institutional Investor* criterion emerges. In several subcategories distribution is modestly more concentrated (see table 16), perhaps because the number of firms seen as fully qualified to "run the books" in a public financing is smaller or because some of the clients undertook no public financing during the five years before 1978.

The distribution of total corporate relationships as measured by the lead manager criterion is as follows:

Goldman, Sachs	12.1%	Salomon Brothers	10.2%
Merrill Lynch	11.9%	Lehman Brothers	9.4%
Morgan Stanley	11.4%	First Boston	9.2%

Noteworthy here and in the subsequent breakdowns using the lead manager criterion is the appearance of the same firms that dominated in the *Institutional Investor* list presented in table 14. The concentration figures for total corporate relationships are almost identical to those for the *Institutional Investor* list. Approximately 46 percent of the relationships are held by the top four firms and 75 percent are held by the top eight firms.

In the industrial category, many of the same firms appear, and the concentration ratios (46 percent for the top four and 72 percent for the top eight) are also similar to those noted in the *Institutional Investor* classification:

Goldman, Sachs	13.5%	First Boston	7.0%
Morgan Stanley	11.9%	Kidder, Peabody	6.9%
Lehman Brothers	10.7%	Smith Barney	6.6%
Merrill Lynch	9.6%		

In the commercial banking category, the following firms have the largest shares:

Salomon Brothers	26.2%
First Boston	16.7%
Lehman Brothers	11.9%

Noteworthy here is Salomon Brothers as top firm in the place of Merrill Lynch, which in lead managership terms held only a 4.8 percent market share, compared to its 19.4 percent share using the

Institutional Investor criterion. Table 16 shows a modestly higher degree of concentration using the lead manager criterion than under the *Institutional Investor* classification.

Salomon Brothers' prominent position in financial industry-related corporate issuers is further reinforced by the figures for diversified financial company relationships:

Salomon Brothers   26.1%
Merrill Lynch   17.4%
Goldman, Sachs   13.0%

Salomon retains its place from the *Institutional Investor* list, but Goldman Sachs supplants Blyth Eastman in third place. It is noteworthy that concentration is greater for diversified financial companies here (65 percent for the top four and 87 percent for the top eight firms) than is generally true for other categories (table 16).

In retailing relationships, the same firms appear under the lead manager criterion as under the *Institutional Investor* criterion:

Goldman, Sachs   33.3%
Merrill Lynch   14.8%
First Boston   11.1%
Lehman Brothers   11.1%

Concentration in the retailing sector is the highest of any of the groupings used in this examination, measured by either the *Institutional Investor* list (71.4 percent for the top four firms and 85.8 percent for the top eight) or the lead manager criterion (76.3 percent for the top four and 92.5 percent for the top eight).

The pattern in the transportation sector is also basically similar to that revealed using the *Institutional Investor* list criterion:

Salomon Brothers   26.3%
Lehman Brothers   15.8%
Goldman, Sachs   10.5%
E. F. Hutton   10.5%
Morgan Stanley   10.5%

Using this criterion, Bache and First Boston lose relative position, whereas E. F. Hutton and Morgan Stanley gain.

The pattern in the utilities market sector revealed by the lead manager criterion also agrees with the *Institutional Investor* list findings, except for modestly greater concentration shown in table 16 (67 percent for the top four and 87 percent for the top eight):

Merrill Lynch	24.0%
Morgan Stanley	16.0%
First Boston	14.7%
Salomon Brothers	12.0%

This list includes the same group (with the addition of Salomon Brothers) that stood out in the list based on the *Institutional Investor* criterion.

B   Logit Analysis: Variables and Statistical Results

This appendix expands upon the text's discussion of the logit analysis results reported in tables 20 and 21. Here we define each variable used in the logit analysis, state our hypothesis about the variable's effect on the probability of a match, and summarize some of the more interesting statistical results obtained. While the discussion of the results is based upon a review of all of the logit runs, the reader is reminded that no single run included all the variables discussed below.

The Variables

1. Average rank of the bank's clients

Description: In each of the six broad categories of companies studied, the rank of client was first translated into a number between 1 and 100. An industrial that ranks 346th (by sales) out of 500 would get the rank 69.2; the 34th out of 50 utilities would have the rank 68, and so on. The variable then indicates the average rank of all a bank's clients. It partially indexes the bank's quality and prestige in corporate finance. Thus, a positive coefficient is expected for the average rank variable.

Statistical outcome: Generally, the coefficient of the average rank of clients, using either the *Institutional Investor* criterion or the lead manager criterion, is not statistically significant. Apparently, having large clients does not in itself attract other corporate clients. The discussion of the next variable helps explain this finding.

2. Rank distance

Description: This variable is the absolute value of the difference between the client's rank and the average rank of the bank's clients. It is included because we suspect that the underwriting market is segmented to some extent by client size. Thus, we hypothesize that the smaller the rank distance, the more likely is a match between investment bank and client. The sign of the coefficient should be negative.

Statistical outcome: The coefficient of the rank distance variable was negative and significant in both tables. Thus, the closer a prospective client's size is to the average size of the bank's existing client base, the more likely it is that the client will use that bank. And the further a corporation is in size from the investment bank's average, the less likely it is that the company will be a client.

3. Average rank of bank's clients times client's rank

Description: this variable was an early attempt to capture information that is better captured by rank distance. Because it treats size asymmetrically, we decided to concentrate on the rank distance variable.

Statistical outcome: See the discussion of the rank distance variable.

4. Merger volume

Description: Data are included on the total assets of the bank's merger clients in 1978 as another partial index of the quality of the corporate finance group. It is well known that merger counseling and brokerage business is highly prized by investment banking firms. The hypothesis is that the ability to generate this business for a particular firm is influenced partly by the quality of the corporate finance professionals who provide the services. Thus, these data provide another measure of corporate finance capability. Our hypothesis, then, was that banks with higher merger volume would be more attractive to all prospective investment banking clients.

Statistical outcome: Merger volume has a positive coefficient; it is statistically quite significant in table 21, which uses the lead manager criterion, but not in table 20, which uses the *Institutional Investor* criterion. This result is consistent with our understanding of the mergers and acquisitions advisory business. This business tends to be dominated by a few firms, most of which are also distinguished by leadership in the public underwriting business. This suggests that these lead managers also have the most highly qualified mergers and acquisitions professionals. These banks' prominence in mergers and acquisitions may attract underwriting business, and vice versa.

5. Total research score

Description: Each year *Institutional Investor* publishes the results of a poll in which portfolio managers evaluate and rank U.S. securities analysts who cover each of approximately 40 industries. First-, second-, and third-place and runner-up analysts are chosen. We awarded a bank four points for each first-place analyst it employed, three points for each second-place analyst, two points for each third-place analyst, and one point for each runner-up. The total research score assigned to each investment bank is the sum of all research points scored by that bank's analysts. We hypothesize that strong research competence attracts institutional investors as clients of the bank's research services and that this institutional following will attract investment banking clients that hope to appeal to institutional investors. Total research score might also serve as a general measure of the bank's overall quality.

Statistical outcome: The coefficient of total research score was generally not significant. The general insignificance of the coefficient is not very surprising, in light of the indirect mechanism through which it might have been expected to attract investment banking clients.

6. Research score times the fraction of client's equity held by institutional investors

Description: This variable combines the overall research score of the bank (which was studied in isolation as variable 5) with the fraction of the prospective client's equity that is held by institutional investors. The rationale for testing this variable is similar to that for the previous variable. If research capability is an important marketing tool, and if its impact is greater on institutional investors, then that capability may be of greater interest to firms whose stock tends to be held by institutional investors.

Statistical outcome: The results here are similar to those obtained for total research score. A bank's general research strength apparently does not attract clients even when the prospective client is in large part owned by institutional investors.

7. Bank's research score in client's industry

Description: This variable measures the bank's research expertise only in the prospective client's specific industry. The clients were categorized into 30 industries using the assignments made by *Fortune.* Each bank's research score in each industry was calculated, using the same scoring system as was used to calculate total research score. Thus, this variable sums the bank's total research points in the industry in which the potential client is located. We hypothesize that it partially measures a bank's expertise in that industry.

We reasoned that a bank's research expertise in a particular industry might attract corporate clients from that industry. For example, a bank's research analysts might be used to build greater competence among business and corporate finance professionals. (Any reciprocal transmission of confidential or inside information from the corporate finance professionals to the research analysts might be legally prohibited. To prevent this illegal flow of information, securities firms have a so-called Chinese Wall between research and corporate finance to guard against the inherent conflicts of interest in these buying and selling roles.)

Statistical outcome: The coefficient of this variable is positive, and is marginally significant in some specifications. It appears that investment banks do use their research competence in particular industries as a tool for attracting corporate clients from those industries. This result raises questions about the impermeability of the Chinese Wall.

8. Share of the assets in the corporation's industry managed by the bank

Description: This is meant to measure the extent to which a bank's underwriting dominance, or at least a leading position, in a particular industry attracts additional clients from that industry.

We hypothesize that in some industries clients may be attracted by such expertise. On the other hand, the sensitivity of proprietary information in some industries may cause just the opposite effect if a bank seeks additional clients in the same industry.

Our method of calculating the variable deserves explanation. Take the petroleum industry as an example. Exxon is a client of Morgan Stanley. This variable for the Morgan Stanley–Exxon pair is the total assets of Morgan Stanley's oil industry clients, excluding Exxon, divided by the total assets of all oil industry clients of the 20 banks, again excluding Exxon. Thus, the variable is a market share by assets, excluding the particular corporation whose choice is being estimated. We leave out the corporation whose choices are being studied to avoid having a component of the dependent variable on the right-hand side. This would be a particularly significant problem if the corporation was large in its industry.

Statistical outcome: A bank's industry share as measured for the analysis is positive and sometimes significant in table 21 and always positive and very significant in table 20. This disparity may be explained by the tendency of some issuers to turn to a smaller cadre of recognized underwriting leaders for underwriting regardless of the leaders' share of the issuers' industries (table 21), but to rely on other investment banks for other services (table 20). For some of these other services, such as mergers and acquisitions advising, a bank's knowledge of the client's industry—as evidenced by the bank's share of that industry—may be more essential.

9. Number of corporate finance professionals

Description: This variable is the number of corporate finance professionals employed by each bank. Since capacity to acquire and hold clients is in part a function of adequate staffing, the hypothesis is that the larger the staff, the more clients the bank will acquire.

Statistical outcome: The coefficient of this variable is positive and very significant in table 20 (*Institutional Investor* criterion) and positive and significant, but less so, in table 21 (lead manager criterion). It appears, therefore, that expanding the corporate finance group generates new investment banking business but not necessarily (or so surely) lead manager positions in public offerings.

Two strategic lessons can be drawn from comparing tables 20 and 21. First, new investment banking business can be generated by expanding corporate finance resources, a strategy that has been used by a number of traditional distribution firms in recent years. Second, a comparison of tables 20 and 21 suggests a limitation on the effectiveness of this strategy; it enables firms to acquire certain types of additional business, but not necessarily to acquire lead managerships. Moreover, we suspect that the quality differentials in the staffs of competing banks also have a significant impact on the acquisition of new clients and that these differentials are not captured by a variable that measures sheer size of staff.

10. Number of clients per corporate finance professional
Description: This variable is the total number of clients divided by the number of corporate finance professionals employed by a bank. It represents an effort to discriminate among the staffs of competing investment banking firms on the basis of perceived overall quality. The hypothesis is that highly skilled professionals with a corporate following will attract inordinate amounts of business to their sponsoring firms; thus, the size of this variable increases with overall quality. The coefficient of this variable should be positive.
Statistical outcome: The results support this hypothesis.

11. Number of retail brokerage representatives in the United States
Description: Some investment banks are also sizable securities brokerage houses. One of the best measures of retail distribution capacity is the number of retail representatives employed. The hypothesis is that this capacity should be helpful in predicting the acquisition of investment banking clients because in-house retail distribution capability provides added assurance to corporate clients that new financings will be placed successfully.
Statistical outcome: The number of retail representatives is an interesting variable. In table 20 (*Institutional Investor* criterion) its coefficient is generally negative but marginally significant. In table 21 (lead manager criterion) the coefficient is generally negative and significant. The negative and significant sign probably results from a negative correlation between the number of retail representatives and some unmeasured aspect of quality. Since the re-

tail brokerage firms are relative newcomers to underwriting, the number of retail representatives probably correlates negatively with experience and with underwriting prestige; the process of building a reputation in corporate finance and underwriting is a lengthy one. This correlation with an unobserved variable knocks down the coefficient in each table; their relative sizes are as expected.

12. Number of retail representatives times one if the corporation is a utility, times zero otherwise
Description: This variable tests the hypothesis that utilities have more interest in a bank's retail distribution capacity than do other firms in the sample. Their interest would stem from the fact that their securities appeal primarily to individual investors.

Statistical outcome: The coefficient of this variable is positive and very significant, confirming our hypothesis that retail distribution capability is particularly valued by utilities. Apparently utility clients find the value of captive in-house retail distribution sufficiently compelling to influence the probability of directing lead managerships as well as general corporate finance business to these banks.

13. Number of retail representatives times the fraction of the corporation's stock held by noninstitutional investors
Description: This variable is used to test the hypothesis that a corporate issuer whose stock is held predominantly by individuals will gravitate toward an investment bank with relatively extensive in-house retail distribution capability.

Statistical outcome: The results do not support the hypothesis. In table 20 (*Institutional Investor* criterion), the coefficients are not significant. In table 21 (lead manager criterion), most of the coefficients are not significant. In specification 2, the coefficient is significant but negative, probably because the "total retail representatives" variable was omitted. The present variable, which has as a factor the number of retail representatives, probably picked up the negative impact (observed earlier) of that omitted variable.

14. Number of institutional brokerage representatives
Description: The hypothesis is that the larger the institutional sales force and, by implication, the more substantial the commit-

ment of resources to this important market segment, the more likely the firm will be to attract corporate clients.

Statistical outcome: The coefficients of this variable are not significant in table 20, but are significant and positive in table 21. This difference is explained by the difference between vying for corporate client business in general and competing for lead managerships in particular. Each of the firms in our study has at least a modest institutional sales force; for many client services such as mergers and acquisitions, lease financing, and private placements (usually marketed by corporate finance professionals), no more than this minimum institutional sales capacity is needed.

Table 21, however, deals with firms that are able to attract lead managerships in corporate underwritings. These firms typically devote large amounts of resources to maintaining a competitive edge in the institutional market. It is not surprising, therefore, to find that a larger institutional sales force helps to attract underwriting clients.

15. Number of institutional representatives times the fraction of the corporation's equity held by institutional investors

Description: The hypothesis is that companies whose shares are largely held by institutions will gravitate toward investment banks with relatively extensive in-house institutional distribution capabilities.

Statistical outcome: The coefficients of this variable were not statistically significant. Apparently, having in-house institutional distribution capacity does not help banks to attract companies whose securities are held largely by institutional investors.

16. Average assets of the bank's clients

Description: This variable measures the same effect as variable 1 (average rank of the bank's clients). The hypothesis is that large clients enhance a firm's prestige and therefore aid the bank in attracting additional clients.

Statistical outcome: The coefficient of this variable is almost always positive, and it is always positive when it is significant. As expected, the prestige of having large clients does help draw additional clients. These results, when contrasted with those for variable 1, indicate that clients' absolute size, rather than their relative size within their respective categories, is important.

17. Share of 1978 negotiated debt dollar volume

Description: This variable is defined as the proportion of total negotiated debt financings managed by a particular bank. It is a market share figure that captures experience in debt issues, an attribute that might appeal to clients who issue a lot of debt or who require expertise in structuring and timing debt issues.

Statistical outcome: In most specifications the coefficient is negative, but only occasionally is it significant. It may be that an unmeasured variable is distorting the results.

18. Share of negotiated debt times the corporation's bond rating

Description: This variable is defined as the share of negotiated debt multiplied by a numerical value assigned to the potential client's bond rating. The hypothesis is that the most creditworthy issuers will be attracted to investment banks with leading positions in the negotiated debt financing area.

Statistical outcome: Unfortunately, a coding error eliminated bond ratings as a measurable variable.

19. Share of 1978 negotiated equity dollar volume

Description: This variable is defined as the proportion of total negotiated equity financings managed by a particular bank. It is a market share figure that captures experience in equity issues, an attribute that might appeal to clients who issue a lot of equity or who require expertise in structuring and timing equity issues.

Statistical outcome: The coefficients of this variable are not statistically significant. In other words, a banking firm's leading position in negotiated equity financings does not appear to attract additional corporate clients.

20. Share of 1978 total dollar volume of all corporate securities

Description: This variable is defined as the proportion of total debt and equity offerings managed by a particular investment bank. The variable is a market share figure that captures experience in managing public offerings, an attribute that appeals to clients who issue securities or who require expertise in structuring and timing securities issues.

Statistical outcome: The coefficients of this variable are negative and significant in table 20 and generally not significant in table 21. This result is somewhat surprising, especially in light of the fact that the dollar volume summaries published by *Institutional Investor* receive considerable attention among investment bankers and their clients.

21. Share of 1978 competitive securities times one if client is a utility, times zero otherwise
Description: This variable tests our hypothesis that utilities are more concerned with a bank's share of competitive underwritings than are nonutilities. This concern is expected because lead managerships in utility offerings are often determined by competitive bid; in contrast, lead managerships in other corporate offerings are typically determined by negotiation.
Statistical outcome: The coefficients of this variable are generally positive and very significant. As expected, utilities are attracted to investment banks with a leading position in competitive bid financings.

22. Share of total debt times corporation's bond rating
Description: This variable is defined as the share of total competitive and negotiated debt offerings multiplied by a numerical value assigned to the potential client's bond rating. The hypothesis is that the most creditworthy issuers will be attracted to investment banks with leading positions in the debt financing area.
Statistical outcome: Unfortunately, a coding error eliminated bond ratings as a measurable variable.

23. Share of negotiated debt times the corporation's leverage times the corporation's growth rate
Description: This variable is defined as the share of total negotiated debt offerings multiplied by both the potential client's leverage position, defined as $1 - $ (net worth/assets), and its five-year growth rate in average sales. The hypothesis is that corporate issuers with the fastest-growing capital needs and greatest tendencies to utilize debt financing will be attracted to (and be attractive to) investment banks with leading positions in underwriting negotiated debt.
Statistical outcome: In most specifications the coefficients are negative; in table 21 they are always negative and sometimes significant. One interpretation of this result is that the leading underwriters of debt are not particularly interested in highly

leveraged, fast-growing firms whose securities might seem somewhat speculative.

24. Number of international corporate finance professionals times the fraction of the corporation's sales outside the United States

Description: This variable is the product of the number of international corporate finance professionals multiplied by the fraction of a client company's sales outside the United States. The hypothesis is that corporations with substantial international business will be attracted to investment banks with corporate finance resources outside the country.

Statistical outcome: These coefficients are statistically insignificant. Apparently the number of international corporate finance professionals does not systematically affect potential clients' choice of an investment banker, even when the prospective clients have substantial foreign sales.

25. Number of international brokerage representatives times the fraction of the corporation's sales outside the United States

Description: This variable is the product of the number of international brokerage representatives multiplied by the fraction of a client company's sales outside the United States. The hypothesis is that corporations with substantial international business will be attracted to investment banks with professional sales resources outside the country.

Statistical outcome: The coefficients are generally not significant. Apparently foreign brokerage sales capacity has no observable impact on internationally oriented clients' choice of an investment banker.

26. Dummies for specific investment banks

Description: In some of the versions of the model, we included dummy variables for the major investment banks on the ground that these banks may have unmeasured attributes that influence corporate choices.

Statistical outcome: The coefficients from dummy variables, when they are included, tend to be consistently negative and statistically significant. This reflects the presence of unobserved factors in the marketplace—factors that are correlated with the larger firms.

C Tabulation of Bank-Client Relationships, 1970

This privately compiled list was provided by a cooperating investment banking firm. It includes only the *Fortune* 500 industrial companies. Each comanager received full credit. Credit for corporate relationships was based on latest negotiated public offering (researched at least as far back as 1950). In the absence of an offering, credit was based on directorships, publicly acknowledged representation in a merger, or other financial advisory assignment.

General Motors	Morgan Stanley
Standard Oil (N.J.)	Morgan Stanley
Ford Motor	Goldman Sachs
General Electric	Goldman Sachs, Morgan Stanley
International Business Machines	Morgan Stanley
Chrysler	First Boston, Merrill Lynch, Lazard
Mobil Oil	Morgan Stanley
Texaco	Morgan Stanley
International Tel. & Tel.	Kuhn Loeb, Lazard
Gulf Oil	First Boston
Western Electric	Goldman Sachs, First Boston, Salomon, Merrill Lynch
U. S. Steel	Morgan Stanley
Standard Oil of California	Blyth, Dean Witter
Ling-Temco-Vought	Goldman Sachs, Lehman Bros.

DuPont (E.I.) de Nemours	Morgan Stanley
Shell Oil	Morgan Stanley
Westinghouse Electric	Kuhn Loeb, First Boston
Standard Oil (Ind.)	Morgan Stanley
General Telephone & Electronics	Paine Webber, Stone & Webster, Mitchum
Goodyear Tire & Rubber	Dillon Read
RCA	Lazard, Lehman Bros.
Swift	Salomon, White Weld
McDonnell Douglas	Lehman Bros.
Union Carbide	Morgan Stanley
Bethlehem Steel	Kuhn Loeb, Smith Barney
Boeing	First Boston
Eastman Kodak	Morgan Stanley
Procter & Gamble	Goldman Sachs
Atlantic Richfield	Smith Barney
North American Rockwell	Kuhn Loeb
International Harvester	Morgan Stanley
Kraftco	Goldman Sachs
General Dynamics	Lazard, E. F. Hutton
Tenneco	White Weld, Stone & Webster, Paine Webber
Continental Oil	Morgan Stanley
United Aircraft	Drexel
Firestone Tire & Rubber	Drexel
Phillips Petroleum	First Boston
Litton Industries	Lehman Bros., Clark Dodge
Armour	Merged
Lockheed Aircraft	Blyth
Caterpillar Tractor	Lehman Bros., Merrill Lynch
Monsanto	Dillon Read, White Weld, Lazard
Occidental Petroleum	Lehman Bros.
Singer	Morgan Stanley, Goldman Sachs
General Foods	Goldman Sachs, Lehman Bros.
Sun Oil	Smith Barney, Eastman Dillon
Rapid-American	Allen, CBWL-Hayden Stone, Cantor
Dow Chemical	Smith Barney
Grace (W. R.)	Merrill Lynch, Paine Webber
Continental Can	Golden Sachs, Lehman Bros.
International Paper	First Boston

Burlington Industries	Kidder Peabody
Borden	Morgan Stanley
Boise Cascade	Blyth
American Can	Morgan Stanley
Textron	Merrill Lynch
Union Oil of California	Dillon Read
Minnesota Mining & Manufacturing	Goldman Sachs, Kidder Peabody, Lazard
Sperry Rand	Eastman Dillon
TRW	Smith Barney
Reynolds (R.J.) Tobacco	Dillon Read, Reynolds
Armco Steel	Goldman Sachs, Smith Barney
Gulf & Western Industries	Lehman Bros., Salomon, Kidder Peabody
Cities Service	First Boston, Loeb Rhoades
Uniroyal	Kuhn Loeb
Aluminum Co. of America	First Boston
Consolidated Foods	None
Republic Steel	First Boston, Merrill Lynch
AMK	Goldman Sachs, Hornblower
Xerox	First Boston
Bendix	Blyth
U.S. Plywood-Champion Papers	Goldman Sachs, Eastman Dillon
Signal Companies	Merrill Lynch, duPont Glore Forgan
Honeywell	Eastman Dillon
Anaconda	First Boston
FMC	Lehman Bros., Kidder Peabody
Ralston Purina	Goldman Sachs, Kidder Peabody
Coca-Cola	Morgan Stanley
American Brands	Morgan Stanley, Goldman Sachs
Allied Chemical	Lazard, Lehman Bros., Loeb Rhoades
American Standard	Blyth
Beatrice Foods	Kidder Peabody
Teledyne	CBWL-Hayden Stone
Owens-Illinois	Lazard, Goldman Sachs
Raytheon	Paine Webber
National Cash Register	Dillon Read
Celanese	First Boston
Weyerhauser	Morgan Stanley
Goodrich (B.F.)	Goldman Sachs

National Steel	Merrill Lynch, First Boston, Kuhn Loeb
CPC International	Dillon Read
Inland Steel	Kuhn Loeb
American Home Products	Lehman Bros.
Genesco	White Weld
Grumman	Dillon Read
Standard Oil (Ohio)	Morgan Stanley
Georgia-Pacific	Blyth
Olin	Eastman Dillon, Wertheim
Whirlpool	Lazard, Goldman Sachs
Ashland Oil & Refining	Dillon Read, Eastman Dillon
PPG Industries	First Boston
Colgate-Palmolive	Dillon Read
Getty Oil	Eastman Dillon, Kuhn Loeb, Lehman Bros.
U. S. Industries	Goldman Sachs, Smith Barney
General Tire & Rubber	Kidder Peabody
American Cyanamid	White Weld
Borg-Warner	Goldman Sachs, duPont Glore Forgan, Hornblower
Ogden	Allen, Wertheim
Eaton Yale & Towne	Merrill Lynch
Kennecott Copper	Morgan Stanley, Kuhn Loeb
Deere	Drexel
Mead	Smith Barney, Goldman Sachs
Reynolds Metals	Dillon Read
Stevens (J.P.)	Goldman Sachs
Martin Marietta	Blyth
Carnation	Kidder Peabody
White Motor	Blyth
PepsiCo	Allen
Standard Brands	Lehman Bros.
Norton Simon	Goldman Sachs
National Lead	Kuhn Loeb
Bristol-Myers	Goldman Sachs, Lehman Bros.
Lykes-Youngstown	Smith Barney, Bear Stearns
Kaiser Aluminum & Chemical	First Boston, Dean Witter
Marathon Oil	First Boston
Crown Zellerbach	Lehman Bros.
Amerada Hess	Dillon Read
Avco	Lehman Bros.
General Mills	Dillion Read

Campbell Soup	First Boston
Motorola	Goldman Sachs
St. Regis Paper	White Weld
Kimberly-Clark	Morgan Stanley
Texas Instruments	Morgan Stanley
Combustion Engineering	First Boston
SCM	Eastman Dillon
Warner-Lambert Pharmaceutical	Morgan Stanley, Eberstadt
Pfizer (Chas.)	Eberstadt
Allis-Chalmers Manufacturing	Blyth
Studebaker-Worthington	Goldman Sachs, Lehman Bros.
Heinz (H.J.)	Morgan Stanley
Walter Kidde	Goldman Sachs
American Smelting & Refining	None
Philip Morris	Goldman Sachs, Lehman Bros.
White Consolidated Industries	Lehman Bros.
American Metal Climax	Lehman Bros.
Whittaker	Smith Barney
Burroughs	Kidder Peabody, Lehman Bros.
Hercules	Lehman Bros.
Pullman	First Boston
American Motors	Lehman Bros.
Illinois Central Industries	Salomon
Scott Paper	Smith Barney, Drexel, Merrill Lynch
Colt Industries	None
International Utilities	Goldman Sachs
National Biscuit	Lazard
Northwest Industries	None
Babcock & Wilcox	Morgan Stanley
Ingersoll-Rand	Morgan Stanley, Smith Barney
Dart Industries	Lehman Bros., Merrill Lynch, Paine Webber
Interco	Goldman Sachs, duPont Glore Forgan
Dresser Industries	First Boston, Eastman Dillon
National Distillers & Chemical	Dominick, duPont Glore Forgan
United Merchants & Manufacturers	Lehman Bros.
Zenith Radio	None
Iowa Beef Packers	New York Securities, First Nebraska
Phelps Dodge	Morgan Stanley

Anheuser-Busch	Dillon Read
Johnson & Johnson	Morgan Stanley
Del Monte	Dean Witter
Avon Products	Morgan Stanley, Hornblower
Dana	Merrill Lynch
Merck	Goldman Sachs
Clark Equipment	Blyth
Squibb Beech-Nut	Wertheim
Emerson Electric	None
Hormel (Geo. A.)	None
Jim Walter	Becker, Loeb Rhoades
Time Inc.	None
Pet	Lehman Bros.
Gillette	Morgan Stanley, White Weld
McGraw-Edison	Dean Witter
GAF	Blyth, First Boston
American Machine & Foundry	Eastman Dillon
Lear Siegler	None
Johns-Manville	Morgan Stanley
Control Data	White Weld, Kidder Peabody
Pillsbury	Goldman Sachs, Paine Webber
Oscar Mayer	Smith Barney
Budd	Smith Barney
Otis Elevator	First Boston
Northrop	Blyth, duPont Glore Forgan
Central Soya	Goldman Sachs
Quaker Oats	Goldman Sachs, White Weld, Lazard
Armstrong Cork	Kidder Peabody, Smith Barney, First Boston
Essex International	Paine Webber
Crane	Dominick
North American Phillips	Morgan Stanley
Sterling Drug	Eastman Dillon
Agway	None
Kellogg	Morgan Stanley, duPont Glore Forgan, Clark Dodge
Diamond Shamrock	Goldman Sachs, Kuhn Loeb
Magnavox	None
Eli Lilly	None
Fruehauf	Merrill Lynch
Allegheny Ludlum Steel	First Boston, Smith Barney

Carrier	Drexel
Koppers	First Boston
Corning Glass Works	Goldman Sachs, Lazard
Evans Products	Goldman Sachs
Ethyl	Blyth
Wheeling-Pittsburgh Steel	Shearson Hammill, First Boston
International Minerals & Chemical	White Weld
Stauffer Chemical	Morgan Stanley
Diamond International	Kidder Peabody
Sherwin-Williams	Morgan Stanley
Lever Brothers	Hallgarten
Liggett & Myers	White Weld
Owens-Corning Fiberglas	Goldman Sachs, Lazard, White Weld
Air Reduction	Morgan Stanley
American Sugar	Goldman Sachs
Cluett, Peabody	Goldman Sachs, Lehman Bros.
Cerro	Morgan Stanley
Seagram (Joseph E.) & Sons	Goldman Sachs, Loeb Rhoades
Kerr-McGee	Lehman Bros., Dempsey
Pacific Car & Foundry	Morgan Stanley
U. S. Gypsum	None
Polaroid	Kuhn Loeb
Brunswick	Goldman Sachs, Lehman Bros.
Union Camp	Eastman Dillon
Libbey-Owens-Ford	Lazard
Rohm & Haas	Drexel, Kidder Peabody
Scovill Manufacturing	Smith Barney
Castle & Cooke	First Boston
Kayser-Roth	Hornblower
Indian Head	White Weld
Eltra	White Weld
Farmland Industries	None
Kaiser Steel	First Boston
Tecumseh Products	Hornblower
Westvaco	Drexel
Schlitz (Jos.) Brewing	Goldman Sachs
Addressograph Multigraph	Smith Barney
Cummins Engine	First Boston
Pennwalt	Kidder Peabody

Universal Oil Products	Lehman Bros., Merrill Lynch, Smith Barney
Abbott Laboratories	Goldman Sachs, Lehman Bros.
Collins Radio	Kidder Peabody, White Weld
Timken Roller Bearing	Hornblower
McGraw-Hill	Smith Barney, duPont Glore Forgan
Ward Foods	Lehman Bros.
Brown Shoe	Goldman Sachs
Land O'Lakes	None
Crowell Collier & Macmillan	Loeb Rhoades
Times Mirror	Goldman Sachs, Paine Webber, White Weld, Kidder Peabody, Salomon
Loew's Theatres	Lazard
A-T-O	Eastman Dillon
Kelsey-Hayes	Goldman Sachs
Lowenstein (M.) & Sons	Eastman Dillon
West Point-Pepperell	White Weld
Sunbeam	Goldman Sachs, Wm. Blair
Upjohn	Morgan Stanley
Crown Cork & Seal	duPont Glore Forgan
General Cable	Paine Webber, Warburg
City Investing	Lehman Bros.
Revere Copper & Brass	Eastman Dillon
DiGiorgio	Dean Witter
Hygrade Food Produts	Weis, Voison
Ex-Cell-O	None
USM	First Boston
Smith (A.O.)	Goldman Sachs
Admiral	duPont Glore Forgan
Cudahy	None
National Industries	Hornblower
Hammermill Paper	Morgan Stanley
Norton	Lehman Bros.
Libby, McNeill & Libby	Goldman Sachs
National Gypsum	E. F. Hutton
Gould	Goldman Sachs, Laird
Richardson-Merrell	Smith Barney
Harris-Intertype	Kidder Peabody, McDonald
International Milling	Kidder Peabody

Potlatch Forests	None
Purex	Blyth
Flintkote	Lehman Bros.
Bemis	Goldman Sachs
Bangor Punta	White Weld, Warburg
Inmont	Dillon Read
Outboard Marine	Morgan Stanley
Interlake Steel	Kuhn Loeb
Fuqua Industries	Bache
Hewlett-Packard	Blyth
Dayco	Lehman Bros.
Archer Daniels Midland	Kidder Peabody
Revlon	Lehman Bros., Rothschild
Smith Kline & French Laboratories	Smith Barney, Drexel
Hershey Foods	None
Fairchild Hiller	Lehman Bros.
Mohasco Industries	Morgan Stanley
National Can	Bear Stearns, Smith Barney
American Bakeries	Merrill Lynch
Hoover	None
Donnelley (R.R.) & Sons	Merrill Lynch
General American Transportation	Kuhn Loeb
Alco Standard	Merrill Lynch
Heublein	Goldman Sachs, duPont Glore Forgan
Morton-Norwich Products	Goldman Sachs
Reliance Electric	Merrill Lynch, Lehman Bros.
Sunstrand	White Weld, Hornblower
Sybron	Merrill Lynch, Lehman Bros.
Dan River Mills	Kidder Peabody
Cannon Mills	Kidder Peabody
Bell & Howell	None
Staley (A.E.) Manufacturing	Lehman Bros.
Chemetron	Merrill Lynch
Apex	Blyth, Lazard
Curtiss-Wright	None
Cotton Producers Association	None
Campbell Taggart Associated Bakeries	None
Pitney-Bowes	First Boston
Lipton (Thomas J.)	None

Levi Strauss	Lehman Bros., Dean Witter
Fairchild Camera & Instrument	None
Jonathan Logan	Goldman Sachs
Lone Star Cement	CBWL-Hayden Stone, Lazard
Howmet	Lazard
Cyclops	Lehman Bros.
General Instrument	Loeb Rhoades
Insilco	Lehman Bros.
Murphy Oil	Morgan Stanley
Koehriag	None
Thiokol Chemical	Kidder Peabody, Lehman Bros., Eastman Dillon
Interstate Brands	White Weld
American Beef Packers	Pressprich
Joy Manufacturing	First Boston
Kellwood	Goldman Sachs, Lehman Bros.
Questor	None
Emhart	Drexel
Texas Gulf Sulphur	Morgan Stanley
New York Times	First Boston
Wallace-Murray	Reynolds
Hoerner Waldorf	Blyth
Witco Chemical	Goldman Sachs, Smith Barney
American Petrofina	Blyth, Hornblower, White Weld
Square D	First Boston
Trane	Smith Barney
ESB	Smith Barney
Kendall	First Boston, Goldman Sachs
Warnaco	Lehman Bros.
Chesebrough-Pond's	Lehman Bros.
Maremont	Kuhn Loeb
Cutler-Hammer	Morgan Stanley
Eagle-Picher Industries	Goldman Sachs
Black & Decker Manufacturing	Lehman Bros.
Missouri Beef Packers	duPont Glore Forgan
Allied Products	Hornblower
Air Products & Chemicals	Kuhn Loeb
McLouth Steel	First Boston
DeSoto	Goldman Sachs
Spring Mills	Morgan Stanley
Cincinnati Milling Machine	Eastman Dillon
Carborundum	First Boston

Porter (H.K.)	First Boston
National Service Industries	None
Coastal States Gas Producing	First Boston, Kuhn Loeb, Paine Webber
Fairmont Foods	Blyth
I-T-E Imperial	None
Cessna Aircraft	Kidder Peabody
Norris Industries	None
Miles Laboratories	White Weld
Cone Mills	Morgan Stanley
Clark Oil & Refining	Kuhn Loeb, Loewi
Champion Spark Plug	Merrill Lynch
Midland-Ross	Lehman Bros., Smith Barney
U. S. Shoe	Merrill Lynch
Diversified Industries	New York Securities
Chromalloy American	Goldman Sachs
Chicago Bridge & Iron	None
Parke, Davis	Merged
Harsco	Lehman Bros.
Anchor Hocking	Dillon Read
ACF Industries	duPont Glore Forgan
Rockwell Manufacturing	Kuhn Loeb
Great Western United	None
Allied Mills	None
Stokely-Van Camp	Reynolds
Rohr	First Boston, Lester Ryon
Rath Packing	None
NVF	Shaskan
Federal-Mogul	Goldman Sachs
Amsted Industries	Hornblower
Spencer Packing	None
Stanley Works	Blyth
American Enka	Drexel
Simmons	White Weld
Bunker-Ramo	Hornblower, Allen
Pabst Brewing	Bear Stearns
Fedders	Allen, duPont Glore Forgan, Hornblower
Avnet	Kuhn Loeb
Vulcan Materials	Goldman Sachs
Needham Packing	Cruttenden Podesta
Rex Chainbelt	Morgan Stanley

Certain-Teed Products	None
Todd Shipyards	Blyth
Schering Plough	Merrill Lynch
Eastern Gas & Fuel Associates	First Boston
Republic	Bear Stearns
Federal Co.	None
AMP	Kidder Peabody, Blyth
Mattel	Goldman Sachs, Smith Barney
Phillips-Van Heusen	Goldman Sachs
Fieldcrest Mills	Blyth
Sheller-Globe	Shields
Grolier	Smith Barney, Dominick
Handy & Harman	Goldman Sachs
Becton, Dickinson	Eberstadt
Roper	Goldman Sachs
Collins & Aikman	Lehman Bros.
Houdaille Industries	Allen
Commercial Metals	Eppler
Blue Bell	First Boston
Gerber Products	None
American Chain & Cable	None
General Host	Allen, Kleiner Bell
Armstrong Rubber	Goldman Sachs
Hobart Manufacturing	None
Penn-Dixie Cement	Bear Stearns
Robertson (H.H.)	First Boston
Perkin-Elmer	Blyth
VF	Eastman Dillon
Parker-Hannifin	Kidder Peabody
Gardner-Denver	Hornblower, Becker
Automation Industries	Eastman Dillon
Nebraska Consolidated Mills	First Nebraska
Signode	Goldman Sachs
Bath Industries	Goldman Sachs
Beech Aircraft	White Weld
Cabot	White Weld, Loeb Rhoades
Sanders Associates	Kidder Peabody, Lehman Bros.
Stewart-Warner	duPont Glore Forgan
Varian Associates	Dean Witter
General Signal	None
Inland Container	Lazard
Ceco	Hornblower

Interpace	Goldman Sachs
Riegel Paper	Morgan Stanley
Easco	Hornblower
Keystone Consolidated Industries	Eastman Dillon, Hornblower
Fibreboard	Lehman Bros., Dean Witter
Green Giant	Paine Webber
Commonwealth Oil Refining	First Boston
Skyline	Rodman & Renshaw
Reichold Chemicals	Blyth
St. Joseph Lead	None
Hyster	Morgan Stanley
American Hoist & Derrick	Lehman Bros.
Cooper Industries	White Weld
Trans Union	Salomon
Hanna Mining	First Boston
Great Northern Paper	Lehman Bros.
Freeport Sulphur	None
U.S. Smelting, Refining & Mining	Bear Stearns
Rheingold	Loeb Rhoades
Wean United	duPont Glore Forgan
Arvin Industries	Hornblower
Keebler	Goldman Sachs
Brockway Glass	Lehman Bros., Blyth
Briggs & Stratton	Robert Baird
Cowles Communications	Goldman Sachs
Max Factor	Blyth
Federal Pacific Electric	Hornblower
Ludlow	Arthur Wood
Johnson Service	Robert Baird
Schaefer (F.&M.)	White Weld
Granite City Steel	First Boston, Merrill Lynch, Eastman Dillon
Triangle Industries	Eastman Dillon
Willamette Industries	Blyth
Hoover Ball & Bearing	Goldman Sachs
Wrigley (Wm.) Jr.	None
American Biltrite Rubber	Goldman Sachs
Warner & Swasey	Blyth
American Forest Products	Merged
Warwick Electronics	Merged
Western Publishing	Goldman Sachs
Maytag	Eastman Dillon, Merrill Lynch

Microdot	White Weld
Reeves Brothers	Lehman Bros.
Instrument Systems	Shaskan
Nekoosa-Edwards Paper	Merged
National Presto Industries	Bache, Eberstadt
Peter Eckrich & Sons	Merged
Searle (G.D.)	Smith Barney
Amerace Esna	Salomon
Carpenter Technology	None
Knight Newspapers	Goldman Sachs
Olivetti Underwood	None
Lubrizol	Morgan Stanley
Farmers Union Central Exchange	None
Monfort of Colorado	Faulkner, Walston

Tables

Table 1 Top 20 underwriting firms, 1950–1980.[a]

Firm	1950 Rank	1950 Volume	1955 Rank	1955 Volume	1960 Rank	1960 Volume	1965 Rank	1965 Volume	1970 Rank	1970 Volume	1975 Rank	1975 Volume	1980 Rank	1980 Volume
Merrill Lynch	4	339	15	203	5	609	4	1,342	2	6,398	1	14,066	1	21,298
Salomon Brothers	11	145	16	202	18	144	7	924	4	4,589	3	11,884	2	17,213
First Boston	3	556	2	894	1	1,340	1	2,362	1	7,023	2	12,198	3	12,701
Morgan Stanley	2	645	1	1,019	3	970	5	1,101	5	4,094	4	11,226	4	11,668
Goldman, Sachs				—	16	180	11	707	8	2,905	5	8,502	5	11,058
Lehman Brothers	7	233	8	441	4	610	2	1,706	3	5,101	7	6,450	6	10,246
Blyth Eastman	6	265	4	748	6	603	3	1,549	6	4,019	6	7,141	7	9,262
Kidder Peabody	5	289	11	301	8	374	8	825	9	2,864	9	5,768	8	9,082
Dean Witter	—	—	19	101	20	143	12	610	13	1,393	11	4,256	9	6,770
E. F. Hutton	—	—	—	—	—	—	—	—	—	—	15	2,596	10	5,420
Lazard Frères	—	—	18	142	19	143	9	799	14	1,327	18	1,704	11	4,659
Bache	—	—	—	—	—	—	—	—	—	—	—	—	12	4,621
Smith Barney	—	—	9	321	—	—	14	508	12	2,155	10	4,333	13	4,051
Warburg	—	—	—	—	—	—	—	—	—	—	—	—	14	3,668
Dillon, Read	12	121	12	271	12	230	18	242	16	1,270	17	2,135	15	3,534
Drexel Burnham	18	41	—	—	—	—	—	—	19	899	16	2,210	16	2,939
Shearson			—	—	17	159	—	—	—	—	—	—	17	2,451
Bear, Stearns	—	—	—	—	—	—	—	—	—	—	—	—	18	2,413
Rothschild, Unterberg	—	—	—	—	—	—	—	—	—	—	—	—	19	2,364
Donaldson, Lufkin	—	—	—	—	—	—	—	—	—	—	—	—	20	1,452
Halsey, Stuart	1	724	3	868	2	1,097	13	591	7	3,077	8	6,201		—
Paine Webber		—		—	13	205	17	362	15	1,273	12	3,719		—
Kuhn, Loeb	14	97	6	472	9	357	10	768	18	1,145	13	3,568		—
White, Weld	8	210	7	458	7	578	6	1,050	10	2,629	14	3,552		—

Firm												
Loeb, Rhoades	—	—	—	—	—	—	—	—	—	—	19	1,504
A. E. Ames & Co.	—	—	—	—	—	—	—	—	—	—	20	1,129
Eastman Dillon	10	—	20	94	11	308	—	—	—	—	—	—
Stone & Webster	—	170	14	206	10	310	16	423	11	2,543	—	—
duPont Glore Forgan	—	—	—	—	—	—	15	439	17	1,246	—	—
Equitable Securities	17	51	17	—	—	—	19	185	20	718	—	—
Harriman, Ripley	13	102	5	163	14	200	20	176	—	—	—	—
Glore, Forgan	15	79	10	493	15	184	—	—	—	—	—	—
Alex Brown & Sons	—	—	13	302	—	—	—	—	—	—	—	—
Union Securities	9	183	—	264	—	—	—	—	—	—	—	—
Wood, Gundy	16	61	—	—	—	—	—	—	—	—	—	—
Harris, Hall	19	34	—	—	—	—	—	—	—	—	—	—
Blair, Rollins	20	34	—	—	—	—	—	—	—	—	—	—

Source: Investment Dealer's Digest.

a. Full credit was given to all managers of comanaged offerings. In many cases, firms disappear from the top 20 because they merged into other firms. Volume figures are in millions of dollars.

Table 2 Dollar volume concentration: Negotiated securities.[a]

	1972	1973	1974	1975	1976	1977
Negotiated debt						
Top 4 $	8.2	6.9	19.9	31.8	27.1	19.7
%	43	41	47	46	50	52
Top 8 $	13.1	11.4	29.5	47.9	37.2	27.9
%	68	68	69	70	69	74
Top 15 $	17.2	15.3	38.7	62.0	47.8	34.0
%	90	91	91	90	89	90
Total universe $	19.2	16.8	42.7	68.6	53.6	37.8
Negotiated equity						
Top 4 $	6.1	5.9	3.0	9.2	9.0	7.7
%	39	36	45	47	47	50
Top 8 $	9.0	10.0	4.4	14.4	14.4	11.3
%	58	62	67	73	76	74
Top 15 $	12.3	14.0	5.6	18.4	17.7	14.1
%	79	86	85	94	94	93
Total universe $	15.5	16.2	6.5	19.7	18.9	15.3
Negotiated debt and equity						
Top 4 $	14.3	12.3	22.5	41.0	36.7	27.4
%	42	39	46	46	50	52
Top 8 $	22.0	21.2	33.6	62.3	50.0	38.5
%	66	67	69	70	68	74
Top 15 $	28.6	28.3	44.0	80.4	65.8	46.9
%	85	89	91	91	90	90
Total universe $	33.6	31.6	48.4	88.2	73.3	52.0

Source: Volume data from *Institutional Investor.*

a. "Universe" refers to the top 25 firms. All dollar figures are in billions. Full credit was given to all managers of comanaged offerings.

Table 3 Dollar volume concentration: Competitive securities.[a]

	1972	1973	1974	1975	1976	1977
Competitive debt						
Top 4 $	11.0	10.8	12.4	9.5	10.2	14.1
%	38	38	38	34	33	27
Top 8 $	18.4	18.8	20.8	16.2	17.7	25.9
%	64	65	63	57	57	49
Top 15 $	25.3	26.0	29.0	24.6	26.6	43.3
%	88	91	83	87	85	82
Total universe $	28.8	28.7	33.0	28.2	31.2	52.7
Competitive equity						
Top 4 $	2.8	2.8	1.3	1.6	3.0	4.2
%	39	30	35	31	26	30
Top 8 $	4.7	5.3	2.0	2.9	5.6	7.3
%	66	57	56	55	49	53
Top 15 $	6.5	8.0	3.0	4.4	9.1	11.3
%	91	86	83	85	80	82
Total universe $	7.2	9.2	3.6	5.2	11.3	13.7
Competitive debt and equity						
Top 4 $	13.6	13.2	13.7	11.0	11.9	18.2
%	38	35	38	33	28	27
Top 8 $	22.4	22.8	22.6	18.8	21.9	32.7
%	62	60	62	56	52	49
Top 15 $	31.3	33.6	31.8	29.0	34.6	53.1
%	88	89	87	87	82	80
Total universe $	35.8	37.7	36.4	33.2	42.0	66.3

Source: Volume data from *Institutional Investor.*

a. "Universe" refers to the top 25 firms. All dollar figures are in billions. Full credit was given to all managers of comanaged offerings.

Table 4 Dollar volume concentration: Negotiated and competitive securities.[a]

	1972	1973	1974	1975	1976	1977
Negotiated and competitive debt						
Top 4 $	18.3	16.6	28.5	39.8	36.1	32.8
%	40	38	38	42	43	37
Top 8 $	31.1	29.5	48.0	62.3	52.6	52.2
%	67	67	64	65	63	59
Top 15 $	42.2	40.1	66.1	84.4	72.9	75.1
%	91	91	89	88	88	85
Total universe $	46.3	44.1	74.4	95.6	83.2	87.9
Negotiated and competitive equity						
Top 4 $	8.3	8.1	4.1	10.4	10.7	11.0
%	38	33	44	43	37	39
Top 8 $	13.1	14.4	6.3	16.6	18.3	17.6
%	61	58	68	68	62	62
Top 15 $	18.1	21.1	8.4	22.4	25.5	24.2
%	84	85	90	92	87	86
Total universe $	21.6	24.9	9.3	24.2	29.3	28.1
Negotiated and competitive debt and equity						
Top 4 $	25.7	24.7	32.3	50.2	47.1	44.0
%	38	36	38	42	42	38
Top 8 $	43.2	43.2	53.8	79.0	70.6	69.5
%	63	63	64	66	62	60
Top 15 $	59.6	61.1	75.5	107.0	98.5	99.6
%	87	89	90	89	87	85
Total universe $	68.6	68.4	83.9	120.0	113.0	116.5

Source: Volume data from *Institutional Investor.*

a. "Universe" refers to the top 25 firms. All dollar figures are in billions. Full credit was given to all managers of comanaged offerings.

Table 5 Regression analysis of concentration in underwriting dollar volume, 1972–1977.[a]

Dependent variable	Negotiated				Competitive				Negotiated and Competitive			
	Constant	Time	Volume	R²	Constant	Time	Volume	R²	Constant	Time	Volume	R²
Debt												
C4	39.7 (17.4)	1.55* (3.42)	.027 (.515)	.800	46.2 (18.4)	−1.523* (−3.508)	−.185 (−1.887)	.937	35.2 (9.149)	−1.079 (−1.83)	.112 (1.583)	.428
C8	66.9 (48.8)	1.2* (4.42)	−.037 (−1.176)	.833	73.85 (20.8)	−2.162* (−3.522)	−.207 (−1.498)	.929	67.9 (32.7)	−1.814* (−5.11)	.036 (.948)	.912
C15	106.2 (7.029)	3.127 (1.044)	−.918* (−2.60)	.629	92.5 (18.19)	−.120 (−.136)	−.167 (−.838)	.342	93.1 (75.6)	−1.03* (−4.89)	−.011 (−.501)	.935
Equity												
C4	37.48 (7.83)	2.157* (3.80)	−.092 (−.33)	.783	39.13 (9.57)	−.783 (−1.06)	−.509 (−1.122)	.477	45.2 (10.07)	.820 (1.39)	.410* (−2.149)	.573
C8	53.67 (11.3)	3.07* (5.45)	.230 (.828)	.886	64.29 (16.97)	−2.235* (−3.167)	−.025 (−.059)	.742	68.98 (15.3)	.923 (1.56)	−.404 (−2.12)	.583
C15	73.07 (17.5)	2.357* (4.766)	.449 (1.839)	.873	89.8 (21.7)	−.663 (−.889)	−.280 (−.611)	.304	90.1 (22.9)	1.038 (2.01)	−.277 (−1.657)	.576
Debt and equity												
C4	37.25 (9.65)	1.247 (1.835)	.067 (.952)	.624	42.9 (11.77)	−1.79* (−2.918)	−.08 (−.715)	.861	27.75 (11.148)	−1.297* (−3.656)	.166* (4.817)	.853
C8	65.3 (23.4)	.735 (1.517)	.013 (.264)	.441	68.78 (19.99)	−1.978* (−3.406)	−.116 (−1.096)	.903	58.56 (22.65)	−1.638* (−4.44)	.107* (3.00)	.832
C15	85.56 (41.14)	.553 (1.533)	.033 (.89)	.553	94.33 (21.18)	−2.33 (−.311)	−.177 (−1.292)	.547	89.24 (25.0)	−.397 (−.784)	0 (.013)	.247

a. Cn denotes the n-firm concentration ratio. The numbers in parentheses are t-statistics. Coefficients whose associated t-statistic exceeds 2.132 are significant at the 95 percent level. These coefficients are starred.

Table 6 Dollar revenue concentration: Combined negotiated and competitive securities.[a]

		1970	1971	1972	1973	1974	1975	1976	1977
Debt									
Top 4	$	44	42	29	17	66	83	81	64
	%	32	30	32	36	47	42	42	42
Top 8	$	74	71	52	30	95	131	124	103
	%	53	50	56	62	68	66	64	67
Top 15	$	111	109	73	43	125	174	171	148
	%	80	77	79	89	89	88	88	92
Total universe	$	139	141	92	48	140	198	194	153
Equity									
Top 4	$	48	83	76	40	42	87	71	73
	%	44	31	29	30	49	41	39	46
Top 8	$	73	137	134	71	62	137	112	107
	%	67	51	51	53	72	65	62	67
Top 15	$	106	201	203	107	83	188	161	146
	%	97	75	77	80	93	89	89	92
Total universe	$	109	268	263	134	86	211	181	159
Debt and equity									
Top 4	$	83	110	96	60	100	160	135	128
	%	33	27	27	33	44	39	36	41
Top 8	$	139	192	167	96	143	250	218	200
	%	55	47	47	53	63	61	58	64
Top 15	$	202	298	270	144	197	356	315	284
	%	80	73	76	79	87	87	84	91
Total universe	$	253	408	355	182	227	409	375	312

Source: Securities and Exchange Commission data released to the authors.
a. "Universe" refers to the top 25 firms. All dollar figures are in millions.

Table 7 Regression analysis of concentration in underwriting revenue, 1970–1977.[a]

	Dependent variable	Constant	Time	Revenue	R^2
Debt	C4	27.4	1.9*	.013	.656
		(5.6)	(2.57)	(.361)	
	C8	51.7	2.61*	− .019	.767
		(11.6)	(3.8)	(− .585)	
	C15	79.3	2.257*	− .03	.790
		(27.8)	(4.26)	(− 1.16)	
Equity	C4	46.9	1.043	− .073*	.574
		(5.88)	(1.12)	(− 2.18)	
	C8	70.2	1.042	− .077*	.597
		(8.88)	(1.129)	(− 2.32)	
	C15	98.8	.699	− .087*	.614
		(12.4)	(.754)	(− 2.60)	
Debt and equity	C4	35.37	1.916*	− .028	.636
		(5.29)	(2.768)	(− 1.45)	
	C8	54.04	2.156*	− .024	.645
		(7.59)	(2.93)	(− 1.17)	
	C15	78.0	2.155*	− .017	.732
		(13.75)	(3.67)	(1.06)	

a. Cn denotes the n-firm concentration ratio. The numbers in parentheses are t-statistics. Coefficients whose associated t-statistic exceeds 1.943 are significant at the 95 percent level. These coefficients are starred.

Table 8   Industry-acknowledged groupings of securities firms.[a]

Large investment banks		National wirehouse firms
Special bracket	Other	
The First Boston Corporation	Bear, Stearns & Co.	Bache Halsey Stuart Shields, Inc.
Goldman, Sachs & Co.	Blyth Eastman Dillon & Co., Inc.	Dean Witter Reynolds, Inc.
Merrill Lynch, Pierce, Fenner & Smith, Inc.	Dillon, Read & Co., Inc.	Drexel Burnham Lambert, Inc.
Morgan Stanley & Co., Inc.	Kidder, Peabody & Co., Inc.	E. F. Hutton & Company, Inc.
Salomon Brothers	Lazard Frères & Co.	Loeb Rhoades, Hornblower & Co.
	Lehman Brothers Kuhn Loeb, Inc.	Paine, Webber, Jackson & Curtis, Inc.
		Shearson Hayden Stone, Inc.
		Smith Barney, Harris Upham & Co., Inc.
		Warburg Paribas Becker, Inc.

Source: Securities Industry Association, Securities and Exchange Commission, various syndicate data.

a. The designations "large investment bank" and "national wirehouse firm" have been developed by the Securities Industry Association in cooperation with the securities firms involved; they have been adopted by the Securities and Exchange Commission for their studies and reviews. Designation as a special bracket firm was verified from various prospectuses and tombstone announcements published in recent years. Merrill Lynch, although an acknowledged member of the special bracket category, continues to list itself in the SIA roster as a national wirehouse firm. (In subsequent tables, firm names will be abbreviated.)

Table 9 Comparison of corporate finance staffs for selected securities firms, 1965, 1978.

Firm	Number of corporate and municipal finance professionals, end of 1965	Number of corporate and municipal finance professionals, beginning of 1978	Percentage increase
Bache	24	42	75
Bear, Stearns	10	22	120
Blyth Eastman	35	122	249
Dillon, Read	34	72	112
E. F. Hutton	8	90	1,025
First Boston	25	182	628
Goldman, Sachs	42	156	271
Kidder, Peabody	41	133	224
Merrill Lynch	19	240	1,163
Morgan Stanley	33	135	309
Paine, Webber	12	79	558
Salomon Brothers	10[a]	175	1,650
Smith Barney	36	127	253
Entire group	329	1,575	379

Source: Firms' estimates to authors as of January 1978.

a. Authors' estimate.

Table 10 Branch-office assignment of corporate finance professionals.

Firm	Chicago	Los Angeles	San Francisco	Atlanta	Boston	Houston	Other domestic	Total domestic	Foreign	Total worldwide
Bache	3	0	1	0	0	0	0	4	0	4
Bear, Stearns	0	1	0	0	0	0	0	1	0	1
Blyth Eastman	5	4	4	0	0	0	2	15	13	28
Dean Witter	5	5	14[a]	3	0	2	0	29	4	33
Dillon, Read	2	0	2	0	0	0	0	4	11	15
Drexel Burnham	1	2	0	0	1	0	0	4	2	6
E. F. Hutton	0	7	3	0	1	1	1	13	5	18
First Boston	3	1	1	0	0	0	0	5	30	35
Goldman, Sachs	6	2	2	0	1	1	5	17	10	27
Kidder, Peabody	7	2	2	2	2	2	1	18	0	18
Lehman Brothers	3	2	3	0	0	1	0	9	8	17
Loeb Rhoades	1	1	4	0	0	1	1	8	0	8
Merrill Lynch[b]	12	4	4	2	0	1	0	23	40	63
Morgan Stanley	0	0	0	0	0	0	0	0	17	17
Paine, Webber	4	1	1	2	10	0	1	19	0	19
Salomon Brothers	10	1	3	2	0	0	3	19	4	23
Shearson	0	0	0	0	0	0	1	1	0	1
Smith Barney	5	0	4	0	0	0	1	10	15	25
Warburg	19[a]	3	0	0	0	0	0	22	0	22

Source: Firms' estimates to authors as of January 1978.
a. Historical home office.
b. Includes White Weld.

Table 11   Dollar volume leaders: 10-year comparison.[a]

	1969			1979	
Rank	Firm	Volume ($ millions)	Rank	Firm	Volume ($ millions)
1	First Boston	3,889	1	Salomon Brothers	13,711
2	Merrill Lynch	3,617	2	Merrill Lynch White Weld	13,674
3	Lehman Brothers	3,532	3	First Boston	9,313
4	Salomon Brothers	2,819	4	Goldman, Sachs	6,718
5	Halsey, Stuart	2,561	5	Morgan Stanley	6,705
6	Blyth & Co.	2,457	6	Blyth Eastman Dillon	6,414
7	White, Weld	1,798	7	Kidder, Peabody	5,847
8	Kidder, Peabody	1,644	8	Lehman Brothers Kuhn Loeb	5,789
9	Eastman Dillon, Union Securities	1,638	9	Dean Witter Reynolds	5,375
10	Goldman, Sachs	1,569	10	Bache Halsey Stuart Shields	4,712
11	Morgan Stanley	1,440	11	Smith Barney Harris Upham	4,079
12	Dean Witter	1,028	12	Dillon, Read	3,211
13	Dillon, Read	853	13	Paine, Webber	2,873
14	Smith, Barney	838	14	E. F. Hutton	2,866
15	Paine, Webber	814	15	Drexel Burnham Lambert	2,765
16	Kuhn, Loeb	664	16	Bear, Stearns	2,188
17	Drexel Harriman Ripley	660	17	Lazard Frères	1,825
18	Stone & Webster	604	18	Wertheim & Co.	1,493
19	Hornblower, Weeks	526	19	Warburg Paribas Becker	1,346
20	Shearson Hammil & Co.	399	20	Donaldson, Lufkin & Jenrette	1,119
21	Glore Forgan, W. R. Statts	361	21	Loeb Rhoades, Hornblower	1,076
22	F. I. duPont, A. C. Allyn	354	22	L. F. Rothschild, Unterberg	1,054
23	E. F. Hutton	353	23	Wood Gundy & Co.	1,000
24	Wood Gundy & Co.	299	24	Shearson Loeb Rhoades	888
25	Equitable Securities	296	25	McLoad, Young, Weir	763

Source: *Investment Dealers' Digest* and *Institutional Investor.*
a. Includes negotiated and competitive debt and equity. Full credit was given to all managers of comanaged offerings.

Table 12 Trend in comanagerships in negotiated underwritings, 1974–1977.[a]

| | Utilities and Telephone | | | | | Corporate | | | | | |
| | Sole | | Comanaged | | Total | | Sole | | Comanaged | | Total |
Year	$ Millions	%	$ Millions	%	$ Millions	$ Millions	%	$ Millions	%	$ Millions	$ Millions
1974	2,103	21.2	7,855	78.8	9,959	8,510	54.4	7,139	45.6	15,643
1975	1,844	13.1	12,247	86.9	14,091	15,086	52.5	13,628	47.5	28,714
1976	1,395	12.9	9,368	87.1	10,763	12,988	50.4	12,778	49.6	25,776
1977	1,069	16.6	5,371	83.4	6,441	9,574	43.0	12,691	57.0	22,265

Source: Morgan Stanley & Co., Inc.

a. Includes all debt, equity, and industrial revenue issues.

Table 13 Characteristics of industrial clients, 1978.

Characteristics	Bache	Bear, Stearns	Blyth Eastman	Dean Witter	Dillon, Read	Drexel Burnham	E. F. Hutton	First Boston	Goldman, Sachs	Kidder, Peabody
Institutional Investor criterion										
No. of industrial clients	5	2	34	8	18	2	6	45	96	36
Industrial clients as % of bank's clients	27.8	66.7	66.7	33.3	78.3	40.0	37.5	57.7	75.6	70.6
Share of industrials (n = 542)	.92	.37	6.27	1.48	3.32	.37	1.11	8.30	17.71	6.64
Average sales ($ millions)	636	533	2649	4338	2375	2397	1023	2516	2178	1632
Average assets ($ millions)	475	497	1882	3293	1717	1813	561	2090	1417	1144
Average net income ($ millions)	24	32	128	209	199	62	(11)	101	101	82
Average bond rating[a]	3.5	5.0	3.1	3.3	2.6	3.5	5.3	3.2	2.9	3.0
% foreign sales	3.0	4.0	21.3	27.3	19.9	26.5	8.4	16.4	17.7	22.7
% institutionally held	12.9	22.4	22.7	21.6	21.1	26.0	5.9	25.1	28.6	23.2
Sales growth rate (%)	12.9	20.0	10.9	22.7	15.7	11.6	17.6	13.7	11.1	14.7
Rate of return on assets (%)	4.65	5.40	8.58	6.83	10.70	4.47	(3.04)	5.32	6.85	6.76
Lead manager criterion										
No. of industrial clients	10	15	15	0	12	1	5	21	41	21
Industrial clients as % of bank's clients	71	75	60	0	75	25	56	46	69	75
Share of industrials (n = 303)	3.30	4.95	4.95	0	3.69	0.33	1.65	6.93	13.50	6.93
Average sales ($ millions)	623	981	2546	—	2476	4427	911	3024	3302	1960
Average assets ($ millions)	418	790	1856	—	1867	3396	699	2478	2171	1449
Average net income ($ millions)	23	25	133	—	131	110	(22)	144	169	119
Average bond rating[a]	3.3	3.6	2.8	—	2.6	3.0	5.0	3.1	2.7	2.3
% foreign sales	14.2	15.8	20.0	—	15.2	31.0	3.2	21.4	18.3	27.1
% institutionally held	27.2	23.0	56.8	—	22.2	24.3	9.8	29.4	26.0	26.5
Sales growth rate (%)	12	13	13	—	15	10	13	15	11	15
Rate of return on assets (%)	5	5	8	—	7	3	0	6	8	8

Other attributes

Retail representatives (U.S.)	1990	220	650	3572	0	650	2700	0	65	750
Institutional representatives (U.S.)	82	26	100	35	66	50	100	211	129	105
Brokerage representatives (foreign)	120	12	13	107	6	85	100	34	65	38
Volume of negotiated debt	101	163	717	244	345	374	83	819	2314	461
Volume of negotiated equity	144	163	365	550	61	71	267	485	246	762
Corporate finance professionals	29	21	81	68	44	35	59	110	116	90
Public finance professionals	13	1	28	15	9	1	26	20	23	17
Merger assets	0	0	0	816	200	108	102	1945	1091	102
No. clients commercial banks*	1	0	4	6	0	0	0	10	6	2
No. clients diversified financial*	0	0	5	2	1	0	0	3	2	1
No. clients retailing*	1	1	1	0	0	0	1	2	15	3
No. clients transportation*	5	0	2	0	1	0	2	4	4	0
No. clients utilities*	6	3	5	8	3	3	7	14	4	9
Research score	2	8	14	17	0	29	8	27	50	29

* Institutional Investor criterion.

a. Bond ratings are based on the following scoring system: AAA = 1, AA = 2, A = 3, BAA = 4, BA = 5, B = 6.

Table 13 *Continued*

Characteristics	Lazard Frères	Lehman Brothers	Loeb Rhoades	Merrill Lynch	Morgan Stanley	Paine, Webber	Salomon Brothers	Shearson	Smith Barney	Warburg
Institutional Investor criterion										
No. of industrial clients	30	58	7	68	48	9	22	0	31	17
Industrial clients as % of bank's clients	85.7	69.0	70.0	55.7	68.6	50.0	36.7	0	81.6	77.3
Share of industrials (n = 542)	5.54	10.70	1.29	12.55	8.86	1.66	4.06	0	5.72	3.14
Average sales ($ millions)	2584	2263	1148	2235	6290	783	3884	—	1674	1368
Average assets ($ millions)	2003	1881	1193	1736	4959	677	2904	—	1480	1074
Average net income ($ millions)	109	93	55	102	365	44	178	—	84	73
Average bond rating[a]	2.9	3.2	3.8	3.2	2.3	3.3	2.5	—	2.9	3.6
% foreign sales	23.3	20.6	18.4	18.4	24.6	22.9	18.7	—	18.8	20.3
% institutionally held	27.5	24.5	21.0	25.1	25.9	30.7	21.0	—	26.5	23.2
Sales growth rate (%)	11.1	13.6	12.1	14.3	13.5	15.7	15.7	—	14.8	14.7
Rate of return on assets (%)	6.46	5.63	4.91	5.86	7.19	7.00	6.37	—	8.38	6.64
Lead manager criterion										
No. of industrial clients	13	32	5	29	36	7	18	0	20	2
Industrial clients as % of bank's clients	100	70	83	5	64	64	36	0	95	100
Share of industrials (n = 303)	4.29	10.56	1.65	9.57	11.88	2.31	5.94	0	6.60	.66
Average sales ($ millions)	1553	2453	707	1836	5457	1460	1643	—	1860	1303
Average assets ($ millions)	1286	2198	907	1356	4363	1475	1200	—	1711	1061
Average net income ($ millions)	87	101	39	73	297	75	69	—	134	64
Average bond rating[a]	2.7	3.1	3.3	3.8	2.3	3.0	3.0	—	2.8	3.0
% foreign sales	20.0	20.4	20.0	17.4	24.8	18.7	16.8	—	21.9	21.0
% institutionally held	28.6	26.2	20.6	23.4	27.1	23.1	20.9	—	26.5	29.5
Sales growth rate (%)	13	12	10	13	14	14	16	—	15	15
Rate of return on assets (%)	8	6	5	7	7	6	6	—	11	6

Other attributes

Retail representatives (U.S.)	8	175	2006	6649	65	2080	0	1650	1060	110
Institutional representatives (U.S.)	22	100	111	560	54	125	91	50	58	25
Brokerage representatives (foreign)	7	10	113	406	4	27	NA	70	19	25
Volume of negotiated debt	212	853	228	1248	2603	84	2107	0	666	57
Volume of negotiated equity	0	368	66	1251	690	157	169	13	91	4
Corporate finance professionals	NA	136	51	167	106	56	93	22	80	46
Public finance professionals	NA	12	15	24	0	13	22	3	32	5
Merger assets	2233	1724	247	1602	6088	0	714	0	835	0
No. clients commercial banks*	1	6	0	13	4	1	9	0	1	3
No. clients diversified financial*	0	2	1	3	2	2	7	0	2	0
No. clients retailing*	1	11	1	11	1	2	2	1	1	2
No. clients transportation*	3	5	0	3	2	0	11	0	3	0
No. clients utilities*	0	2	1	24	13	4	9	0	0	0
Research score	0	9	8	76	50	50	9	4	28	2

Table 14 Client distribution by industry, 1978 (*Institutional Investor* criterion).

Firm	% of total corporate relation-ships[a]	% of indus-trials	% of commer-cial banks	% of diver-sified financial	% of retail-ing	% of transpor-tation	% of utilities
Bache	2.0	.9	1.5	0	1.8	10.9	5.4
Bear, Stearns	0.4	.4	0	0	0	2.2	0
Blyth Eastman	6.0	6.3	6.0	15.2	1.8	4.3	4.5
Dean Witter	2.8	1.5	9.0	6.1	0	0	7.1
Dillon, Read	2.7	3.3	0	3.0	0	2.2	2.7
Drexel Burnham	0.6	.4	0	0	0	0	2.7
E. F. Hutton	1.9	1.1	0	0	1.8	4.3	6.3
First Boston	9.1	8.3	14.9	9.1	3.6	8.7	12.5
Goldman, Sachs	14.8	17.7	9.0	6.1	26.8	8.7	3.6
Kidder, Peabody	6.0	6.6	3.0	3.0	5.4	0	8.0
Lazard Frères	4.0	5.5	1.5	0	1.8	6.5	0
Lehman Brothers	9.8	10.7	9.0	6.1	19.6	10.9	1.8
Loeb Rhoades	1.2	1.3	0	3.0	1.8	0	.9
Merrill Lynch	14.3	12.6	19.4	9.1	19.6	6.5	21.4
Morgan Stanley	8.2	8.9	6.0	6.1	1.8	4.3	11.6
Paine, Webber	2.1	1.7	1.5	6.1	3.6	0	3.6
Salomon Brothers	7.0	4.1	13.4	21.2	3.6	23.9	8.0
Shearson	.1	0	0	0	1.8	0	0
Smith Barney	4.4	5.7	1.5	6.1	1.8	6.5	0
Warburg	2.6	3.1	4.5	0	3.6	0	0
No. of relationships	856	542	67	33	56	46	112
C4	48.0	49.9	56.7	54.6	71.4	54.4	53.5
C8	75.2	76.8	86.7	79.0	85.8	82.6	80.3

Source: Data from *Institutional Investor.*
a. Columns may not sum to 100.0% because of rounding.

Table 15 Distribution of clients by industry, 1978 (lead manager criterion).

Firm	% of total corporate relation- ships[a]	% of indus- trials	% of commer- cial banks	% of diver- sified financial	% of retail- ing	% of transpor- tation	% of utilities
Bache	2.9	3.3	4.8	0	3.7	0	1.3
Bear, Stearns	4.1	5.0	0	8.7	7.4	5.3	0
Blyth Eastman	5.1	5.0	9.5	4.3	0	5.3	5.3
Dean Witter	1.2	0	2.4	0	3.7	0	5.3
Dillon, Read	3.3	4.0	0	4.3	0	5.3	2.7
Drexel Burnham	.8	.3	0	0	0	0	4.0
E. F. Hutton	1.8	1.7	0	0	0	10.5	2.7
First Boston	9.2	7.0	16.7	8.7	11.1	5.3	14.7
Goldman, Sachs	12.1	13.5	9.5	13.0	33.3	10.5	0
Kidder, Peabody	5.7	6.9	4.8	4.3	0	0	5.3
Lazard Frères	2.7	4.3	0	0	0	0	0
Lehman Brothers	9.4	10.7	11.9	4.3	11.1	15.8	2.7
Loeb Rhoades	1.2	1.7	0	0	0	0	1.3
Merrill Lynch	11.9	9.6	4.8	17.4	14.8	5.3	24.0
Morgan Stanley	11.4	11.9	9.5	0	7.4	10.5	16.0
Paine, Webber	2.2	2.3	0	4.3	3.7	0	2.7
Salomon Brothers	10.2	5.9	26.2	26.1	3.7	26.3	12.0
Shearson	0	0	0	0	0	0	0
Smith Barney	4.3	6.6	0	4.3	0	0	0
Warburg	.4	.7	0	0	0	0	0
No. of relationships	489	303	42	23	27	19	75
C4	45.6	45.7	64.3	65.2	70.3	63.1	66.7
C8	75.0	72.1	92.9	86.8	92.5	89.5	86.6

Source: Data from Investment Dealers' Digest.
a. Columns may not sum to 100.0% because of rounding.

Table 16 Concentration ratios of client-bank relationships (percentages).

	Total	Industrials	Commercial banks	Diversified financial	Retailing	Transportation	Utilities
Institutional Investor criterion							
Top 4	48.0	49.9	56.7	54.6	71.4	54.4	53.5
Top 8	75.2	76.8	86.7	79.0	85.8	82.6	80.3
Lead manager criterion							
Top 4	45.6	45.7	64.3	65.2	70.3	63.1	66.7
Top 8	75.0	72.1	92.9	86.8	92.5	89.5	86.6

Table 17   Market shares in specific industries.[a]

Firm	Sales 10% +	Sales 20% +	Assets 10% +	Assets 20% +	Income 10% +	Income 20% +	Clients 10% +	Clients 20% +
Bache	2	0	1	1	2	1	4	1
Bear, Stearns	3	2	3	3	4	3	5	3
Blyth Eastman	6	2	7	2	7	3	7	3
Dean Witter	0	0	0	0	0	0	0	0
Dillon, Read	3	2	2	2	3	2	4	2
Drexel Burnham	1	1	1	1	1	1	1	1
E. F. Hutton	1	1	1	0	0	0	2	0
First Boston	7	3	9	3	9	5	9	0
Goldman, Sachs	15	11	15	9	14	12	16	7
Kidder, Peabody	6	3	6	3	8	4	10	3
Lazard Frères	4	1	3	1	4	1	3	2
Lehman Brothers	12	6	13	8	10	8	14	6
Loeb Rhoades	1	0	2	0	0	0	2	1
Merrill Lynch	7	2	7	3	6	3	13	6
Morgan Stanley	13	8	14	9	14	9	15	4
Paine, Webber	0	0	0	0	0	0	1	0
Salomon Brothers	9	5	9	5	10	6	12	7
Shearson	0	0	0	0	0	0	0	0
Smith Barney	5	1	4	1	6	2	9	3
Warburg	1	0	1	1	1	0	1	1

a. The first six columns give, for each investment bank, the number of industries in which a bank's clients account for 10 percent or more (or 20 percent or more) of total sales, assets, or income of all *Fortune* 500 industrial companies in their respective industries. The last two columns give the number of industries in which a bank has 10 percent or more (or 20 percent or more) of all *Fortune* 500 companies in those respective industries. The lead manager criterion was used to determine which banks had which companies as clients. Companies not affiliated with any investment bank were excluded from industry sales, assets, income, and relationships totals. The industries covered are listed in table 29.

Table 18   Stability of bank-client relationships, 1970–1978[a].

Investment bank	No. of clients 1970	No. of clients 1973	No. of clients 1976	No. of clients 1978	No. of clients lost 1970–1973	No. of clients lost 1973–1976	No. of clients lost 1976–1978	No. of clients gained 1973–1976	No. of clients gained 1976–1978
Bache	3	10	20	17	2	5	11	15	8
Bear, Stearns	6	6	7	4	3	3	5	4	2
Blyth Eastman	51	48	60	51	20	19	17	31	8
Dean Witter	11	22	31	24	1	7	15	16	8
Dillon, Read	15	22	29	23	0	2	7	9	1
Drexel Burnham	10	8	6	5	6	4	2	2	1
E. F. Hutton	2	2	14	15	2	0	3	12	4
First Boston	47	56	84	78	7	9	24	37	18
Goldman, Sachs	77	90	122	128	11	15	15	47	21
Kidder, Peabody	26	36	53	51	5	8	16	25	14
Lazard Frères	19	21	33	36	5	5	7	17	10
Lehman Brothers	78	117	102	86	11	42	30	27	14
Loeb Rhoades	27	25	17	10	9	12	7	4	0
Merrill Lynch	52	87	140	121	12	22	46	75	27
Morgan Stanley	53	61	90	69	8	4	28	33	7
Paine, Webber	11	10	16	18	3	5	3	11	5
Salomon Brothers	7	11	48	59	3	2	14	39	25
Shearson	4	6	6	1	1	2	15	2	10
Smith Barney	30	32	39	38	3	8	11	15	10
Warburg	1	7	17	22	1	5	3	15	8
Total	530	677	934	856	113	179	279	436	201

Table 18 Continued

	% lost 1970–1973[b]	% lost 1973–1976	% lost 1976–1978	% new clients 1976[c]	% new clients 1978	Market share 1970[d]	Market share 1973	Market share 1976	Market share 1978
Bache	67	50	55	75	47	.01	.01	.02	.02
Bear, Stearns	50	50	71	57	50	.01	.01	.01	.00
Blyth Eastman	39	40	28	52	16	.10	.07	.06	.06
Dean Witter	09	32	48	52	33	.02	.03	.03	.03
Dillon, Read	00	09	24	31	04	.03	.03	.03	.03
Drexel Burnham	60	50	33	33	20	.02	.01	.01	.01
E. F. Hutton	100	00	21	86	27	.00	.00	.01	.02
First Boston	15	16	29	44	23	.09	.08	.09	.09
Goldman, Sachs	14	17	12	39	16	.15	.13	.13	.15
Kidder, Peabody	19	22	30	47	27	.05	.05	.06	.06
Lazard Frères	26	24	21	52	28	.04	.03	.04	.04
Lehman Brothers	14	36	29	26	16	.15	.17	.11	.10
Loeb Rhoades	33	48	41	24	00	.05	.04	.02	.01
Merrill Lynch	23	25	33	54	22	.10	.13	.15	.14
Morgan Stanley	15	07	31	37	10	.10	.10	.10	.08
Paine, Webber	27	50	19	69	28	.02	.01	.02	.02
Salomon Brothers	43	18	29	81	42	.01	.02	.05	.07
Shearson	25	33	50	33	1000	.01	.01	.01	.00
Smith Barney	10	25	28	38	26	.06	.05	.04	.04
Warburg	100	71	18	88	36	.00	.01	.02	.03
Average	21	26	30	47	23	.05	.05	.05	.05

Table 18   *Continued*

Sources: Privately compiled list of investment banks' corporate clients (see Appendix C), and *Institutional Investor's* annual "Who's With Whom" tabulation.

a. Because the privately compiled list of bank-client relationships used for 1970 included only companies in the industrial category, whereas the three later lists included companies in five additional categories, caution must be exercised in comparing 1970 figures to figures for the later years. Indeed, we do not report "No. of clients gained, 1970–1973" and "% new clients, 1973" because these numbers are particularly difficult to interpret given the expanded list of companies included in 1973 and later years.

The total number of clients indicated in this table may not agree with the totals indicated or implicit in tables 13–17 and 20–33, which generally omit consideration of clients about which data were not complete.

b. Calculated by dividing the number of clients the bank lost 1970–1973 by its number of clients in 1970. The same procedure is followed in the next two columns for 1973–1976 and 1976–1978.

c. Calculated by dividing the number of new clients the bank acquired in 1973–1976 by its number of clients in 1976. The same procedure is followed in the next column for 1976–1978.

d. Market share is defined here as the fraction of total client relationships held by an investment bank in a given year. For example, Bache had 1 percent (.01) of the total client relationships in 1970. This is calculated by dividing the number of clients Bache had in 1970 (3) by the total number of client relationships in 1970 (530).

Table 19 Analysis of client switches.

Investment bank	No. of clients 1970	No. of clients lost 1970–1978	Lost to special bracket firms	Lost to non-special bracket firms	Lost but not to other firms	% lost 1970–1978	No. lost to special bracket firms as % of no. lost to all other firms[a]	% of lost clients going to no other firm
Bache	3	3	0	0	3	100%	—	100%
Bear, Stearns	6	5	0	0	5	83	—	100
Blyth Eastman	51	35	6	6	23	64	50%	66
Dean Witter	11	9	3	0	6	82	100	67
Dillon, Read	15	2	2	0	0	13	100	0
Drexel Burnham	10	9	3	2	4	90	60	44
E. F. Hutton	2	2	1	0	1	100	100	50
First Boston[b]	47	18	4	2	12	38	67	67
Goldman, Sachs[b]	77	26	2	2	22	34	50	85
Kidder, Peabody	26	8	1	0	7	31	100	88
Lazard Frères	19	8	2	0	6	42	100	75
Lehman Brothers	78	41	11	10	20	53	52	49
Loeb Rhoades	27	24	3	2	19	89	60	79
Merrill Lynch[b]	52	25	5	3	17	48	63	68
Morgan Stanley[b]	53	19	3	2	14	36	60	74
Paine, Webber	11	7	1	1	5	64	50	71
Salomon Brothers[a]	7	6	0	2	4	86	0	67
Shearson	4	4	1	1	2	100	50	71
Smith Barney	30	13	0	1	12	43	0	92
Warburg	1	0	0	0	0	0	—	—
Total	530	264	48	34	182	50	59	69
Total for 5 special bracket firms	232	94	14	11	69	41	56	73
Total for 15 others	298	170	34	23	113	57	60	66

Sources: See table 18.

a. The entries in this column equal the number of clients lost to special bracket firms divided by the sum of the number lost to special bracket firms and the number lost to non-special bracket firms.

b. Denotes special bracket firm.

Table 20 Logit model estimates (*Institutional Investor* criterion).[a]

Variable	Specification 1		Specification 2		Specification 3	
	Coefficient	t-statistic	Coefficient	t-statistic	Coefficient	t-statistic
Average rank of clients	—	—	—	—	—	—
Rank distance	—	—	—	—	—	—
Average rank of clients × client's rank	.268	3.92	.261	3.72	.160	2.44
Merger volume	.028	.61	.015	.74	.003	.70
Total research score	−.072	−1.02	—	—	−.023	−.60
Total research score × % of client's equity held by institutions	8.3E-6	.60	1.2E-5	.83	8.1E-6	.59
Bank's research score in client's industry	.001	.05	.020	.73	−4.9E-4	−.02
Share of assets managed in client's industry	2.407	5.07	1.716	3.38	2.292	4.82
No. of corporate finance professionals	.270	3.46	.279	4.56	.134	6.61
Clients per corporate finance professional	.259	4.00	.283	5.05	.156	4.69
No. of retail representatives—domestic	−.033	−.26	—	—	−.013	−.27
No. of retail representatives if client a utility	—	—	—	—	—	—
No. of retail representatives × % of equity not institutionally held	−.001	−.58	−.001	−.50	−.001	−.57
No. of institutional representatives	.018	.37	—	—	−.001	−.20
No. of institutional representatives × % of equity held by institutions	−1.9E-6	−.62	−1.8E-6	−.55	−1.8E-6	−.59
Average assets of bank's clients	.040	.99	.034	1.37	.042	1.76
Share of negotiated debt	—	—	—	—	—	—
Share of negotiated debt × client's bond rating	—	—	—	—	—	—
Share of negotiated equity	—	—	—	—	—	—
Share of total volume	−.140	−1.86	−.160	−2.19	−.024	−1.01

Share of competitive equity × debt if a utility	.007	1.98	.022	3.24	.009	2.53
Share of total debt × client bond rating	—	—	.015	2.02	—	—
Share of negotiated debt × leverage × growth	9.8E-7	.04	−2.0E-5	−.77	1.5E-6	.07
No. of international corporate finance professionals × % of sales foreign	—	—	−.056	−.45	—	—
No. of international representatives × % of sales foreign	—	—	.008	.42	—	—
Dummy variables for First Boston	−1.311	−.99	−.901	−2.25	—	—
Goldman, Sachs	−.854	−1.33	−.833	−1.82	—	—
Lehman Brothers	−1.528	−2.12	−1.192	−3.09	—	—
Merrill Lynch	−1.733	−.87	−1.358	−3.24	—	—
Morgan Stanley	−.804	−.30	−.161	−.12	—	—
Salomon Brothers	.012	.02	—	—	—	—
% correctly predicted	18.22		19.53		16.75	
Likelihood ratio test	566.8		560.7		545.3	
Sample size	13,910		12,130		13,910	

a. Coefficients whose t-statistics exceeds 1.645 are significant at the 95 percent level.

Table 20 *Continued*

Variable	Specification 4		Specification 5		Specification 6	
	Coefficient	t-statistic	Coefficient	t-statistic	Coefficient	t-statistic
Average rank of clients	—	—	.092	.71	−.048	−.42
Rank distance	—	—	−.259	−3.81	−.264	−4.75
Average rank of clients × client's rank	.278	3.91	—	—	—	—
Merger volume	.005	.11	.048	1.19	4.8E-4	.01
Total research score	−.064	−.88	.035	.36	.026	.34
Total research score × % of client's equity held by institutions	1.4E-5	.96	—	—	—	—
Bank's research score in client's industry	.025	.90	.014	.40	0.16	.59
Share of assets managed in client's industry	1.695	3.33	1.710	3.16	2.136	4.42
No. of corporate finance professionals	.329	3.91	.137	2.11	.192	2.55
Clients per corporate finance professional	.268	3.99	.291	3.50	.230	3.52
No. of retail representatives—domestic	.040	.29	−.185	−1.63	.011	.10
No. of retail representatives if client a utility	—	—	—	—	.101	2.49
No. of retail representatives × % of equity not institutionally held	−.001	−.53	—	—	—	—
No. of institutional representatives	−.007	−.14	.033	.71	−.006	−.15
No. of institutional representatives × % of equity held by institutions	−2.0E-6	−.63	—	—	—	—
Average assets of bank's clients	.027	.66	—	—	—	—
Share of negotiated debt	—	—	—	—	—	—
Share of negotiated debt × client's bond rating	—	—	—	—	−7.0E-5	.54
Share of negotiated equity	—	—	—	—	−.139	.56
Share of total volume	−.181	−2.29	—	—	—	—

Share of competitive equity × debt if a utility	.022	3.28	—	—	.006	1.53
Share of total debt × client bond rating	.015	1.93	—	—	—	—
Share of negotiated debt × leverage × growth	− 2.0E-5	− .79	—	—	—	—
No. of international corporate finance professionals × % of sales foreign	− .053	− .42	—	—	—	—
No. of international representatives × % of sales foreign	.008	.38	—	—	—	—
Dummy variables for First Boston	− .662	− .48	− 1.976	− 1.72	− .303	− .29
Goldman, Sachs	− .481	− .74	− 1.858	− 3.03	− 1.090	− 2.22
Lehman Brothers	− 1.327	− 1.80	− 1.178	− 1.71	− .590	− 1.04
Merrill Lynch	− 1.042	− .51	− 2.309	− 1.13	− 1.097	− .64
Morgan Stanley	.722	.26	− 3.390	− 1.54	− .595	− .26
Salomon Brothers	—	—	− .595	− 1.74	− .307	− 1.07
% correctly predicted	19.53		19.63		18.22	
Likelihood ratio test	562.0		432.6		582.7	
Sample size	12,130		9,265		13,910	

Table 20 Continued

Variable	Specification 7 Coefficient	t-statistic	Specification 8 Coefficient	t-statistic	Specification 9 Coefficient	t-statistic	Specification 10 Coefficient	t-statistics
Average rank of clients	− .065	− .59	− .079	− .70	− .078	− .66	− .163	− 1.87
Rank distance	− .262	− 4.75	—	—	− .269	− 4.79	− .264	− 4.82
Average rank of clients × client's rank	—	—	—	—	—	—	—	—
Merger volume	.013	.39	.002	.04	.029	.65	− .005	− 1.06
Total research score	.027	.35	.026	.34	.011	.14	.038	.79
Total research score × % of client's equity held by institutions	—	—	—	—	—	—	—	—
Bank's research score in client's industry	.023	.86	.017	.63	.015	.55	.016	.59
Share of assets managed in client's industry	2.145	4.45	2.200	4.57	2.172	4.48	2.072	4.28
No. of corporate finance professionals	.160	3.07	.191	2.53	.258	2.99	.140	6.07
Clients per corporate finance professional	.229	3.56	.229	3.52	.253	3.65	.149	4.01
No. of retail representatives—domestic	− .025	− .30	.007	.07	− .071	− .60	− .118	− 2.11
No. of retail representatives if client a utility	.114	2.86	.100	2.46	.099	2.45	.094	2.34
No. of retail representatives × % of equity not institutionally held	—	—	—	—	—	—	—	—
No. of institutional representatives	.003	.09	− .005	− .12	.016	.40	− .004	− .58
No. of institutional representatives × % of equity held by institutions	—	—	—	—	—	—	—	—
Average assets of bank's clients	—	—	—	—	—	—	—	—
Share of negotiated debt	—	—	—	—	− 1.200	− 1.56	− .268	− 1.67
Share of negotiated debt × client's bond rating	—	—	− 1.1E-4	− .89	—	—	—	—
Share of negotiated equity	—	—	− .136	− .55	− .248	− .96	.107	.67
Share of total volume	—	—	—	—	—	—	—	—

Share of competitive equity × debt if a utility	—	—	.005	1.36	.006	1.63	.008	2.01
Share of total debt × client bond rating	—	—	—	—	—	—	—	—
Share of negotiated debt × leverage × growth	—	—	—	—	—	—	—	—
No. of international corporate finance professionals × % of sales foreign	—	—	—	—	—	—	—	—
No. of international representatives × % of sales foreign	—	—	—	—	—	—	—	—
Dummy variables for First Boston	-.568	-.62	-.340	-.33	-1.084	-.96		
Goldman, Sachs	-1.139	-2.31	-1.095	-2.23	-.300	-.43		
Lehman Brothers	-.620	-1.09	-.606	-1.06	-1.230	-1.73		
Merrill Lynch	-1.430	-.88	-1.154	-.68	-1.828	-1.05		
Morgan Stanley	-1.353	-.73	-.632	-.28	-.598	-.27		
Salomon Brothers	-.261	-.93	-.286	-1.00	.625	.94		
% correctly predicted	18.46		18.22		18.34		17.85	
Likelihood ratio test	579.8		559.7		584.9		575.0	
Sample size	13,910		13,910		13,910		13,910	

Table 21 Logit model estimates (lead manager criterion).[a]

Variable	Specification 1		Specification 2		Specification 3	
	Coefficient	t-statistic	Coefficient	t-statistic	Coefficient	t-statistic
Average rank of clients	—	—	—	—	—	—
Rank distance	—	—	—	—	—	—
Average rank of clients × client's rank	.632	4.05	.643	3.24	.543	4.11
Merger volume	.092	1.52	.043	1.13	−1.2E-4	−.02
Total reseach score	−.062	−.73	—	—	.029	.43
Total research score × % of client's equity held by institutions	−.001	−.11	−.018	−.76	−8.1E-4	−.08
Bank's research score in client's industry	.005	.14	.046	1.00	.003	.07
Share of assets managed in client's industry	1.246	1.84	.461	.53	1.375	2.06
No. of corporate finance professionals	.117	.82	.350	2.78	.149	4.43
Clients per corporate finance professional	.152	1.25	.181	1.26	.106	1.66
No. of retail representatives—domestic	−.700	−2.70	—	—	−.399	−1.91
No. of retail representatives if client a utility	—	—	—	—	—	—
No. of retail representatives × % of equity not institutionally held	.034	1.28	−.030	−1.58	.033	1.29
No. of institutional representatives	.096	1.41	—	—	.004	.25
No. of institutional representatives × % of equity held by institutions	−.017	−.52	−.067	−1.43	−.019	−.58
Average assets of bank's clients	.045	.82	.101	1.59	−.025	−.55
Share of negotiated debt	—	—	—	—	—	—
Share of negotiated debt × client's bond rating	—	—	—	—	—	—
Share of negotiated equity	—	—	—	—	—	—
Share of total volume	.028	.17	−.175	−1.05	.082	1.43

	Coef.	t	Coef.	t	Coef.	t
Share of competitive equity × debt if a utility	.011	2.47	.030	2.38	.010	2.35
Share of total debt × client bond rating	—	—	4.202	1.46	—	—
Share of negotiated debt × leverage × growth	-.027	-1.49	-.059	-2.20	-.020	-1.24
No. of international corporate finance professionals × % of sales foreign	—	—	1.526	.55	—	—
No. of international representatives × % of sales foreign	—	—	-.578	-1.25	—	—
Dummy variables for First Boston	-3.213	-1.96	-1.338	-1.73	—	—
Goldman, Sachs	-.734	-.78	1.098	1.70	—	—
Lehman Brothers	-1.733	-2.24	-1.564	-1.94	—	—
Merrill Lynch	-2.951	-.94	.805	.58	—	—
Morgan Stanley	-4.780	-1.24	-.905	-.36	—	—
Salomon Brothers	-1.022	-1.34	—	—	—	—
% correctly predicted	18.9		20.0		18.7	
Likelihood ratio test	275.3		232.7		265.7	
Sample size	7,106		4,560		7,106	

a. Coefficients whose t-statistic exceeds 1.645 are significant at the 95 percent level.

Table 21 Continued

Variable	Specification 4		Specification 5		Specification 6	
	Coefficient	t-statistic	Coefficient	t-statistic	Coefficient	t-statistic
Average rank of clients	—	—	.266	1.26	.038	.22
Rank distance	—	—	−.405	−5.73	−.315	−4.51
Average rank of clients × client's rank	.672	3.32	—	—	—	—
Merger volume	.123	1.65	.123	1.94	.077	1.07
Total research score	−.154	−1.18	−.091	−.90	−.153	−1.45
Total research score × % of client's equity held by institutions	5.2E-4	.02	—	—	—	—
Bank's research score in client's industry	.056	1.22	.017	.34	.051	1.25
Share of assets managed in client's industry	.410	.47	.475	.59	.826	1.06
No. of corporate finance professionals	.189	.98	.128	1.57	.261	2.00
Clients per corporate finance professional	.083	.53	.269	2.45	.240	2.25
No. of retail representatives—domestic	−.674	−1.52	−.512	−1.83	−.153	−.65
No. of retail representatives if client a utility	—	—	—	—	.183	2.99
No. of retail representatives × % of equity not institutionally held	.032	.63	—	—	—	—
No. of institutional representatives	.077	.94	.165	2.07	.099	1.47
No. of institutional representatives × % of equity held by institutions	−.013	−.17	—	—	—	—
Average assets of bank's clients	.090	1.36	—	—	—	—
Share of negotiated debt	—	—	—	—	—	—
Share of negotiated debt × client's bond rating	—	—	—	—	−.135	−1.76
Share of negotiated equity	—	—	—	—	−.218	−.43
Share of total volume	−.006	−.03	—	—	—	—

Share of competitive equity × debt if a utility	.030	2.45	—	—	.008	1.68
Share of total debt × client bond rating	2.679	.88	—	—	—	—
Share of negotiated debt × leverage × growth	−.065	−2.35	—	—	—	—
No. of international corporate finance professionals × % of sales foreign	.361	.12	—	—	—	—
No. of international representatives × % of sales foreign	−.412	−.86	—	—	—	—
Dummy variables for First Boston	−3.471	−1.78	−.492	−2.58	−2.611	−1.46
Goldman, Sachs	.016	.01	−1.452	−1.48	−.739	−.87
Lehman Brothers	−2.329	−2.49	−2.307	−2.34	−2.176	−2.41
Merrill Lynch	−2.279	−.63	−6.312	−1.45	−5.237	−1.49
Morgan Stanley	−5.828	−1.22	−6.723	−1.85	−3.647	−.93
Salomon Brothers	—	—	−1.214	−2.18	−.613	−1.15
% correctly predicted	20.4		16.7		18.3	
Likelihood ratio test	236.7		223.5		295.1	
Sample size	4,560		5,202		6,239	

Table 21 *Continued*

Variable	Specification 7 Coefficient	Specification 7 t-statistic	Specification 8 Coefficient	Specification 8 t-statistic	Specification 9 Coefficient	Specification 9 t-statistic	Specification 10 Coefficient	Specification 10 t-statistics
Average rank of clients	−.064	−.44	−.037	−.21	−.061	−.37	.137	1.60
Rank distance	−.319	−5.61	—	—	−.321	−5.65	−.324	−5.68
Average rank of clients × client's rank	—	—	—	—	—	—	—	—
Merger volume	.087	1.67	.076	1.06	.081	1.23	−.004	−.88
Total research score	−.049	−.62	−.159	−1.51	−.032	−.38	−.015	−.33
Total research score × % of client's equity held by institutions	—	—	—	—	—	—	—	—
Bank's research score in client's industry	.049	1.41	.062	1.52	.040	1.11	.039	1.10
Share of assets managed in client's industry	1.540	2.40	.862	1.06	1.247	1.85	1.228	1.84
No. of corporate finance professionals	.156	2.51	.277	2.12	.124	.68	.135	4.48
Clients per corporate finance professional	.317	3.75	.248	2.32	.312	2.83	.152	3.80
No. of retail representatives—domestic	−.097	−.62	−.151	−.64	−.065	−.32	−.160	−2.54
No. of retail representatives if client a utility	.140	2.50	.191	3.12	.140	2.52	.140	2.51
No. of retail representatives × % of equity not institutionally held	—	—	—	—	—	—	—	—
No. of institutional representatives	.134	2.18	.101	1.50	.132	2.00	.003	.23
No. of institutional representatives × % of equity held by institutions	—	—	—	—	—	—	—	—
Average assets of bank's clients	—	—	—	—	—	—	—	—
Share of negotiated debt	—	—	−.191	−2.52	.465	.35	.236	1.31
Share of negotiated debt × client's bond rating	—	—	−.271	−.54	—	—	—	—
Share of negotiated equity	—	—	—	—	.018	.03	.245	1.18
Share of total volume	—	—	—	—	—	—	—	—

	Model 1		Model 2		Model 3		Model 4	
Share of competitive equity × debt if a utility	—	—	.007	1.48	.007	1.58	.007	1.64
Share of total debt × client bond rating	—	—	—	—	—	—	—	—
Share of negotiated debt × leverage × growth	—	—	—	—	—	—	—	—
No. of international corporate finance professionals × % of sales foreign	—	—	—	—	—	—	—	—
No. of international representatives × % of sales foreign	—	—	—	—	—	—	—	—
Dummy variables for First Boston	−3.305	−2.20	−2.637	−1.48	−3.155	−1.86	—	—
Goldman, Sachs	−1.746	−2.19	−.615	−.73	−2.139	−1.54	—	—
Lehman Brothers	−1.971	−2.44	−2.233	−2.47	−1.743	−1.79	—	—
Merrill Lynch	−7.622	−2.17	−5.307	−1.52	−7.713	−2.11	—	—
Morgan Stanley	−5.146	−1.73	−3.384	−.86	−5.415	−1.30	—	—
Salomon Brothers	−.837	−1.89	−.491	−.93	−1.317	−1.14	—	—
% correctly predicted	15.2		17.7		15.6		15.9	
Likelihood ratio test	329.8		274.1		332.5		324.2	
Sample size	8,041		6,239		8,041		8,041	

Table 22.   Actual and predicted market shares.[a]

| Firm | Market Share | |
	Actual	Predicted
Bache	2.82	2.89
Bear, Stearns	4.47	4.47
Blyth Eastman	4.71	4.84
Dean Witter	1.18	1.31
Dillon, Read	3.77	3.71
Drexel Burham	.94	.78
E. F. Hutton	2.12	1.71
First Boston	8.47	8.47
Goldman, Sachs	12.71	12.71
Kidder, Peabody	6.12	6.07
Lehman Brothers	9.65	9.65
Loeb Rhoades	1.41	1.60
Merrill Lynch	13.18	13.18
Morgan Stanley	12.00	12.00
Paine, Webber	2.59	2.71
Salomon Brothers	8.71	8.71
Smith Barney	4.71	4.60
Warburg	.47	.59

[a] Lazard Frères and Shearson were omitted because of limited data.

Table 23 Logit equation used in analysis of groups.

Variable		Coefficient	t-statistic
1	Average rank of clients	− .0858	− .52
2	Rank distance	− .3488	− 5.89
4	Merger volume	.0776	1.04
5	Total research score	.0133	.14
7	Bank's research score in client's industry	.0258	.70
8	Share of assets managed in client's industry	.6562	.89
9	No. of corporate finance professionals	.1958	.97
10	Clients per corporate finance professional	.4040	2.54
11	No. of retail representatives—domestic	− .1019	− .45
12	No. of retail representatives if client a utility	.1290	2.28
14	No. of institutional representatives	.1030	1.29
17	Share of negotiated debt	.4702	.30
19	Share of negotiated equity	.2119	.33
20	Share of total volume	− .1720	− .80
21	Share of competitive equity × debt if a utility	.0117	2.55
23	Share of negotiated debt × leverage × growth	− .2315	− 1.31
26	Dummy variables for First Boston	− 2.936	− 1.51
	Goldman, Sachs	− 1.251	− .87
	Lehman Brothers	− 1.853	− 1.80
	Merrill Lynch	− 6.064	− 1.53
	Morgan Stanley	− 4.149	− .91
	Salomon Brothers	− 0.738	− .61
	% correctly predicted	16.71	
	Likelihood ratio statistic	297.6	
	Sample size	7225	

Table 24 Average predicted concentration ratios for client businesses.

	C1	C2	C3	C4	C5	Herfindahl index (H)[b]	$1/H$
Average concentration	17.21	31.02	41.81	51.04	58.56	.0982	10.57
Standard deviation	5.2	7.46	8.08	8.32	7.99	.0195	3.015
Incremental concentration[a]		13.81	10.79	9.23	7.52		
Actual concentration in overall market	13.18	25.89	37.89	47.54	56.25		

a. The incremental concentration listed under C2 is calculated by subtracting C1 from C2, that listed under C3 by subtracting C2 from C3, and so on.

b. The Herfindahl index has a value of one in an industry controlled by a monopoly, and $1/H$ if the industry contains H firms with equal market shares. Its inverse is sometimes interpreted as the hypothetical number of firms in the industry.

Table 25 Correlation coefficients between predicted probability vectors.

					Group I			
	Bache	Bear, Stearns	E. F. Hutton	First Boston	Kidder, Peabody	Loeb Rhoades	Paine, Webber	Smith Barney
Group I								
Bache	1	.762	.928	.762	.580	.827	.970	.787
Bear, Stearns		1	.867	.913	.883	.985	.835	.965
E. F. Hutton			1	.902	.766	.931	.978	.913
First Boston				1	.910	.942	.841	.965
Kidder, Peabody					1	.876	.679	.904
Loeb Rhoades						1	.896	.979
Paine, Webber							1	.864
Smith Barney								1
Group II								
Merrill Lynch								
Salomon Brothers								
Group III								
Dillon, Read								
Drexel Burnham								
Goldman, Sachs								
Lehman Brothers								
Morgan Stanley								
Warburg								
Group IV								
Blyth Eastman								
Dean Witter								

Group II		Group III						Group IV	
Merrill Lynch	Salomon Brothers	Dillon, Read	Drexel Burnham	Goldman, Sachs	Lehman Brothers	Morgan Stanley	Warburg	Blyth Eastman	Dean Witter
.030	− .021	− .750	− .735	− .691	− .653	− .897	− .606	− .397	− .652
− .465	− .508	− .545	− .402	− .391	− .219	− .684	− .192	− .065	− .466
− .026	− .090	− .787	− .717	− .728	− .602	− .882	− .557	− .248	− .572
− .258	− .291	− .690	− .554	− .543	− .376	− .808	− .363	− .035	− .491
− .401	− .456	− .567	− .300	− .388	− .104	− .706	− .082	− .253	− .217
− .349	− .398	− .635	− .508	− .497	− .343	− .764	− .305	− .109	− .511
− .010	− .065	− .777	− .736	− .710	− .636	− .843	− .589	− .351	− .635
− .331	− .373	− .669	− .528	− .494	− .339	− .776	− .327	− .080	− .521
1	.979	− .378	− .509	− .577	− .628	− .242	− .672	− .205	.009
	1	− .365	− .500	− .504	− .606	− .192	− .671	− .208	− .028
		1	.898	.767	.744	.876	.829	.288	.566
			1	.790	.895	.744	.963	.504	.729
				1	.776	.783	.771	.200	.317
					1	.602	.929	.557	.620
						1	.623	.033	.265
							1	.542	.661
								1	.738
									1

Table 26 Comparison of industry-acknowledged groupings to competitive groups identified by logit analysis.

Industry-acknowledged groupings			Logit analysis
Special bracket origination firms	Other origination firms	National wirehouse firms	Competitive group
First Boston	Kidder, Peabody Bear, Stearns	Paine, Webber Bache E. F. Hutton Loeb Rhoades Smith Barney	I
Merrill Lynch Salomon Brothers			II
Morgan Stanley Goldman, Sachs	Dillon, Read Lehman Brothers	Drexel Burnham Warburg	III
	Blyth Eastman	Dean Witter	IV
	Lazard Frères	Shearson	Not assigned for lack of data

Table 27   Correlation matrix for competitive groups.

Competitive group	Competitive group			
	I	II	III	IV
I	1.0	− .2675	− .7308	− .2594
II		1.0	− .4604	− .1621
III			1.0	.3055
IV				1.0

Table 28   Predicted and actual market shares of the competitive groups.

Group	Market share	
	Predicted	Actual
I	32.5	32.52
II	21.9	21.89
III	39.4	39.44
IV	6.2	6.15
Total	100.0	100.00

Table 29 Group shares of client relationships, by industry, 1978 (*Institutional Investor* criterion).[a]

Industry	Market share				
	Group I	Group II	Group III	Group IV	Unmatched
Mining, oil	0.3125	0.1875	0.3125	0.1875	0.1538
Food	0.2800	0.1400	0.5600	0.0200	0.4219
Tobacco	0.1429	0.1429	0.7143	0.0000	0.0000
Textiles, floors	0.2143	0.0714	0.5714	0.1429	0.2000
Apparel	0.2500	0.0833	0.5000	0.1667	0.1000
Furniture	0.0000	1.0000	0.0000	0.0000	0.5000
Paper, fiber, wood	0.2581	0.1613	0.3548	0.2258	0.2333
Publishing, printing	0.2500	0.5000	0.2500	0.0000	0.5455
Chemicals	0.2264	0.2642	0.4340	0.0755	0.0500
Petro refining	0.2439	0.1707	0.4878	0.0976	0.2121
Rubber, plastic	0.2000	0.0000	0.8000	0.0000	0.1250
Leather	0.0000	0.0000	1.0000	0.0000	0.0000
Glass, concrete	0.1875	0.2500	0.5625	0.0000	0.1333
Metal manufacturing	0.4565	0.1739	0.3261	0.0435	0.1143
Metal products	0.3000	0.1000	0.5500	0.0500	0.2609
Electronics, appliances	0.3548	0.0968	0.5161	0.0323	0.3333
Ships, transportation	0.5000	0.2500	0.0000	0.2500	0.4286
Science & photo equipment	0.4000	0.1333	0.4667	0.0000	0.2667
Motor vehicles	0.1852	0.2222	0.4444	0.1481	0.0952
Aerospace	0.1538	0.2308	0.5385	0.0769	0.2143
Pharmaceuticals	0.2667	0.2667	0.4667	0.0000	0.2353
Soaps, cosmetics	0.0000	0.0000	0.7500	0.2500	0.1250
Office equipment, computers	0.3077	0.1538	0.3077	0.2308	0.1000
Industrial & farm equipment	0.3556	0.2000	0.3556	0.0889	0.2979
Jewelry, silverware	0.0000	0.0000	0.0000	0.0000	0.0000
Music, toys, sport	0.0000	0.0000	1.0000	0.0000	0.5000
Broadcasting, movies	0.0000	0.0000	1.0000	0.0000	0.6667
Beverages	0.1000	0.2000	0.7000	0.0000	0.2222
Commercial banks	0.2239	0.3284	0.2985	0.1493	0.2745
Diversified financials	0.2727	0.3030	0.2121	0.2121	0.5400
Retailing	0.2037	0.2407	0.5370	0.0185	0.3400
Transportation	0.3488	0.3256	0.2791	0.0465	0.4400
Utilities	0.3661	0.2946	0.2232	0.1161	0.1000

a. Horizontal totals may be greater than 1.0000 because a single client may have multiple bank relationships.

Table 30 Group shares of client relationships, by industry, 1978 (lead manager criterion).[a]

Industry	Market share				
	Group I	Group II	Group III	Group IV	Unmatched
Mining, oil	0.3945	0.2909	0.3145	0.0000	0.4362
Food	0.1685	0.0626	0.7689	0.0000	0.4086
Tobacco	0.2668	0.0434	0.6898	0.0000	0.0151
Textiles, floors	0.4319	0.4283	0.0000	0.1398	0.7702
Apparel	0.5510	0.0000	0.3285	0.1204	0.4499
Furniture	0.0000	0.0000	0.0000	0.0000	1.0000
Paper, fiber, wood	0.3385	0.0523	0.4652	0.1440	0.2908
Publishing, printing	0.1994	0.5917	0.2089	0.0000	0.5388
Chemicals	0.2777	0.1129	0.5952	0.0143	0.2423
Petro refining	0.2765	0.0148	0.6021	0.1067	0.4022
Rubber, plastic	0.2501	0.0000	0.7499	0.0000	0.6570
Leather	0.0000	0.0000	0.0000	0.0000	1.0000
Glass, concrete	0.2867	0.1531	0.4851	0.0751	0.3634
Metal manufacturing	0.3113	0.1786	0.5102	0.0000	0.2795
Metal products	0.2960	0.0000	0.6228	0.0812	0.7494
Electronics, appliances	0.1861	0.1491	0.6648	0.0000	0.4224
Ships, transportation	0.2295	0.0465	0.3962	0.3278	0.4816
Science & photo equipment	0.6031	0.0277	0.3692	0.0000	0.4258
Motor vehicles	0.1497	0.1946	0.6523	0.0034	0.0468
Aerospace	0.0515	0.0413	0.9072	0.0000	0.4914
Pharmaceuticals	0.2352	0.0963	0.6686	0.0000	0.4941
Soaps, cosmetics	0.1801	0.0000	0.8199	0.0000	0.4219
Office equipment, computers	0.4052	0.0638	0.1453	0.3857	0.7782
Industrial & farm equipment	0.2129	0.1952	0.5134	0.0784	0.3417
Jewelry, silverware	0.0000	0.0000	0.0000	0.0000	0.0000
Music, toys, sport	0.0000	0.0000	0.0000	0.0000	1.0000
Broadcasting, movies	0.4507	0.0000	0.5493	0.0000	0.5309
Beverages	0.0588	0.3038	0.6375	0.0000	0.3746
Commercial banks	0.2648	0.2786	0.2907	0.1659	0.1240
Diversified financial	0.2265	0.4511	0.2819	0.0406	0.6611
Retailing	0.2139	0.0550	0.7219	0.0092	0.3121
Transportation	0.2170	0.2038	0.5054	0.0738	0.5665
Utilities	0.1320	0.5050	0.2832	0.0799	0.0449

a. Horizontal totals may be greater than 1.0000 because a single client may have multiple bank relationships.

Table 31 Group shares of industry assets, 1978 (*Institutional Investor* criterion).[a]

Industry	Market share				
	Group I	Group II	Group III	Group IV	Unmatched
Mining, oil	0.2392	0.0641	0.2444	0.4523	0.0414
Food	0.2079	0.1712	0.5860	0.0348	0.1850
Tobacco	0.2117	0.0344	0.7539	0.0000	0.0000
Textiles, floors	0.2627	0.0441	0.5035	0.1897	0.0926
Apparel	0.1886	0.0758	0.5425	0.1931	0.0679
Furniture	0.0000	1.0000	0.0000	0.0000	0.4188
Paper, fiber, wood	0.2312	0.1277	0.4238	0.2173	0.1464
Publishing, printing	0.1629	0.6215	0.2156	0.0000	0.4840
Chemicals	0.2428	0.2052	0.4917	0.0603	0.0239
Petro refining	0.1473	0.2719	0.4645	0.1164	0.1376
Rubber, plastic	0.1516	0.0000	0.8484	0.0000	0.0191
Leather	0.0000	0.0000	1.0000	0.0000	0.0000
Glass, concrete	0.2057	0.2109	0.5834	0.0000	0.1161
Metal manufacturing	0.4132	0.1335	0.4054	0.0480	0.0476
Metal products	0.3725	0.0468	0.5593	0.0214	0.2236
Electronics, appliances	0.2073	0.0201	0.7537	0.0189	0.1340
Ships, transportation	0.3585	0.2157	0.0000	0.4258	0.6009
Science & photo equipment	0.2636	0.2612	0.4751	0.0000	0.3764
Motor vehicles	0.1297	0.1529	0.6193	0.0981	0.0121
Aerospace	0.0286	0.3108	0.5973	0.0633	0.1814
Pharmaceuticals	0.2077	0.2246	0.5677	0.0000	0.3057
Soaps, cosmetics	0.0000	0.0000	0.9463	0.0537	0.0340
Office equipment, computers	0.1756	0.1091	0.5726	0.1427	0.0142
Industrial & farm equipment	0.2372	0.2834	0.4202	0.0592	0.2471
Jewelry, silverware	0.0000	0.0000	0.0000	0.0000	0.0000
Music, toys, sport	0.0000	0.0000	1.0000	0.0000	0.7048
Broadcasting, movies	0.0000	0.0000	1.0000	0.0000	0.7181
Beverages	0.0217	0.3448	0.6335	0.0000	0.2583
Commercial banks	0.1783	0.3541	0.2955	0.1722	0.0966
Diversified financial	0.1275	0.3192	0.2758	0.2775	0.4343
Retailing	0.3646	0.1355	0.4943	0.0056	0.1927
Transportation	0.3624	0.3523	0.2514	0.0339	0.2513
Utilities	0.3471	0.2953	0.1916	0.1660	0.3850

a. Horizontal totals may be greater than 1.0000 because a single client may have multiple bank relationships.

Table 32 Group shares of industry assets, 1978 (lead manager criterion).[a]

Industry	Market share				
	Group I	Group II	Group III	Group IV	Unmatched
Mining, oil	0.2857	0.4286	0.2857	0.0000	0.6154
Food	0.3600	0.0800	0.5600	0.0000	0.6250
Tobacco	0.2000	0.2000	0.6000	0.0000	0.2000
Textiles, floors	0.2500	0.5000	0.0000	0.2500	0.7333
Apparel	0.7143	0.0000	0.1429	0.1429	0.4000
Furniture	0.0000	0.0000	0.0000	0.0000	1.0000
Paper, fiber, wood	0.3889	0.1111	0.3333	0.1667	0.4667
Publishing, printing	0.2500	0.5000	0.2500	0.0000	0.6364
Chemicals	0.2759	0.1724	0.5172	0.0345	0.3750
Petro refining	0.4000	0.0500	0.5000	0.0500	0.4545
Rubber, plastic	0.3333	0.0000	0.6667	0.0000	0.7500
Leather	0.0000	0.0000	0.0000	0.0000	1.0000
Glass, concrete	0.3333	0.2000	0.4000	0.0667	0.2667
Metal manufacturing	0.4211	0.2105	0.3684	0.0000	0.5143
Metal products	0.5000	0.0000	0.3750	0.1250	0.6522
Electronics, appliances	0.3913	0.1739	0.4348	0.0000	0.5278
Ships, transportation	0.2500	0.2500	0.2500	0.2500	0.4286
Science & photo equipment	0.5000	0.0833	0.4167	0.0000	0.4667
Motor vehicles	0.2941	0.3529	0.2941	0.0588	0.2857
Aerospace	0.2857	0.1429	0.5714	0.0000	0.5000
Pharmaceuticals	0.3077	0.1538	0.5385	0.0000	0.4118
Soaps, cosmetics	0.3333	0.0000	0.6667	0.0000	0.6250
Office equipment, computers	0.4000	0.2000	0.2000	0.2000	0.5000
Industrial & farm equipment	0.3929	0.1786	0.3214	0.1071	0.4681
Jewelry, silverware	0.0000	0.0000	0.0000	0.0000	0.0000
Music, toys, sport	0.0000	0.0000	0.0000	0.0000	1.0000
Broadcasting, movies	0.4000	0.0000	0.6000	0.0000	0.5000
Beverages	0.1250	0.1250	0.7500	0.0000	0.2222
Commercial banks	0.2558	0.3023	0.3256	0.1163	0.3333
Diversified financial	0.3043	0.4348	0.2174	0.0435	0.6200
Retailing	0.2593	0.1852	0.5185	0.0370	0.5200
Transportation	0.2105	0.3158	0.4211	0.0526	0.6800
Utilities	0.2800	0.3600	0.2533	0.1067	0.1000

a. Horizontal totals may be greater than 1.0000 because a single client may have multiple bank relationships.

Table 33 Profiles of the competitive groups.[a]

Average over firms in group	Group			
	I	II	III	IV
Bank characteristics				
Retail representatives (U.S.)	1350	3324	177	2111
Institutional representatives (U.S.)	102	325	70	67
Foreign representatives	57	406	32	60
Total capital ($ millions)	104	419	70	121
Corporate finance professionals	62	130	80	74
Public finance professionals	17	23	8	21
Merger volume ($ millions)	403	1158	1535	408
Research score	20	42	23	15
Client characteristics				
Sales ($ millions)	1807	2258	2776	2600
Assets ($ millions)	3162	5401	3646	6611
Net income ($ millions)	101	121	146	169
Equity ($ millions)	860	1014	1038	1187
P/E	19	8.5	8.5	7.5
Yield (%)	4.5	4.8	4.4	4.6
Bond rating	2.99	2.88	2.86	2.92
% foreign sales	13.8	14.0	17.5	16.8
% institutionally held	21.5	23.4	24.9	22.4
Sales growth rate (%)	14.26	14.55	12.77	14.11
Leverage	.58	.61	.56	.63
Return on assets	.0518	.0473	.0602	.0631
Return on equity	.1144	.1197	.1236	.1730

a. Table is based on all clients (that is, industrial and others) under *Institutional Investor* criterion. Because "return on assets" (or "return on equity") is not a *weighted* average, it does not necessarily equal "income" divided by "assets" (or "equity"). To illustrate, suppose that a and b are the respective average incomes, and c and d the respective average assets, of the clients of banks 1 and 2. Then $(a/c + b/d)/2$ does not necessarily equal $(a + b)/(c + d)$. The former is analogous to the average returns we report here, the latter to the result of dividing a group's average income by its average assets or equity.

Notes

Introduction

1. Martin Mayer, "Merrill Lynch Quacks like a Bank," *Fortune,* Oct. 20, 1980, p. 134.
2. Securities Industry Association.
3. Ibid.
4. See, for example, Irwin Friend and Marshall E. Blume, "Competitive Commissions on the New York Stock Exchange," *Journal of Finance,* Sept. 1973, pp. 795–819; Securities and Exchange Commission, *Staff Report on the Securities Industry in 1979* (Washington: Directorate of Economic Policy and Analysis, 1980).
5. Phyllis Feinberg, "Investment Banking's Battle of the Bulge," *Institutional Investor,* Jan. 1980, pp. 21–34.

1. Competition: A Historical Sketch

1. Fritz Redlich, *The Molding of American Banking: Men and Ideas,* pt. II (New York: Hafner Publishing, 1951), p. 307.
2. Ibid., p. 318.
3. Ibid., p. 320.
4. Ibid., p. 326.
5. Ibid., p. 321.
6. Vincent P. Carosso, *Investment Banking in America: A History* (Cambridge, Mass.: Harvard University Press, 1970), p. 32.
7. Sheridan A. Logan, *George F. Baker and His Bank, 1840–1955* (Lunenburg: Stinehour Press, 1981), p. 156.
8. Wallace B. Donham, "Underwriting Syndicates and the Purchase and Sale of Securities through Banking Houses" (lecture notes on

"Corporate Finance," Harvard Graduate School of Business Administration, 1908).

9. New York State Legislature, II (Albany: J. B. Lyon Co., 1906), pp. 1021–1022.

10. U.S. Senate, Hearings before the Committee on Finance, 72nd Congress, 1st sess., pt. 1, *Sale of Foreign Bonds or Securities in the United States: Hearings . . . ,* 4 pts. (Washington: 1931–32), pt. 1, p. 23.

11. *New York Times,* Sept. 24, 1905.

12. Adricos H. Joline. "The Method and Conduct of the Reorganization of Corporations" (two lectures delivered at the Harvard Graduate School of Business Administration, April 4 and 6, 1910; copyright A. H. Joline, 1910), p. 58.

13. Carosso, *Investment Banking,* p. 108.

14. U.S. District Court, Southern District of New York (Civil no. 43–757), *United States v. Henry S. Morgan et al.,* p. 629.

15. Ibid., pp. 652, 689, 690.

16. Ibid., pp. 650, 633.

17. Logan, *George F. Baker and His Bank,* p. 142.

18. Carosso, *Investment Banking,* p. 424.

19. Jules I. Bogen, "Changed Conditions in the Marketing of New Issues," *Journal of the American Statistical Association* 33 (March 1938): 34.

20. Carosso, *Investment Banking,* p. 424.

21. Ibid., p. 451.

2. Trends in Concentration

1. Phyllis Feinberg, "Investment Banking's Battle of the Bulge," *Institutional Investor,* Jan. 1980, pp. 21–34.

2. The revenue bond financing part of municipal finance, however, is open only to securities firms under the Glass-Steagall Act. This has become an increasingly important part of the municipal business, and much of the general obligation business is handled via competitive bid. In 1981, 98.5 percent of negotiated municipal financings were revenue-backed. (Source: Kidder, Peabody & Co.)

3. The proportion of total corporate financings arranged in private placement has been generally rising in recent years. See, for instance, Kidder, Peabody & Co., "Private Placements—Market Review 1979," March 1980.

4. See, for instance, annual tabulations in "The 1979 Underwriting Sweepstakes," *Institutional Investor,* March 1980, p. 125.

5. Irwin Friend et al., *Investment Banking and the New Issues Market* (Cleveland: World Publishing Company, 1967), p. 14; Samuel L. Hayes III, "Investment Banking: Power Structure in Flux," *Harvard Business Review,* March–April 1971, p. 136; idem, "The Transformation of

Investment Banking," *Harvard Business Review*, Jan.–Feb. 1979, p. 155; *Institutional Investor*, March 1978, p. 71 (also see period tabulation in *Investment Dealers' Digest*).

6. As noted, the focus here is negotiated underwriting activity. However, because the available revenue data combine the negotiated and the competitive financing results, the results of the analysis of competitive volume are given along with the negotiated data. This will facilitate the analysis of the overall result at the conclusion of this section.

7. By contrast, when regressions were run for the comparable data in the competitively underwritten debt and equity area, the coefficients were significantly negative. Thus, as concentration has *increased* in the negotiated area, concentration has actually *declined* in the competitive area. It may be that as underwriting firms are squeezed out of the negotiated field, they refocus their efforts in the competitive bid area, where each new issue is up for grabs.

8. In a "firm commitment" underwriting, the gross spread is the difference between the public offering price of the underwritten securities and the dollar amount that the underwriters pay the issuer for the shares. Thus, it is the total revenue earned by the investment bankers for their underwriting services. The gross spread is allocated among the investment banks involved in an underwriting according to the degree of participation, with the lead underwriter and comanagers receiving management fees in addition to compensation for their risk-bearing and distributional roles. A selling concession compensates the sales people and makes a contribution toward the overhead of the firm that actually completes the sale. What this revenue measure excludes is the ripple effect of the underwriting on other parts of the firm's business, such as financial services. We discuss this effect later in this book.

9. See, for instance, underwriting activity reported in various issues of *Investment Dealers' Digest*.

10. See, for instance, the lists of financings undertaken during 1973–74, a period of difficult market conditions, as published monthly in the Financing Record department, *Institutional Investor*.

11. See, for instance, Donald F. Turner and Phillip E. Areeda, *Antitrust Law: An Analysis of Antitrust Principles and Their Application*, IV (Boston: Little, Brown, 1980); Dan W. Schneider, "Evolving Proof Standards under Section 7 Mergers in Transitional Markets: The Securities Industry Example," *Wisconsin Law Review*, 1981, no. 1, pp. 1–105.

The U.S. Justice Department is responsible for enforcing the antitrust provisions of the Sherman Act; it scrutinizes horizontal and vertical mergers to test their conformance with it. In implementing the provisions of the Act, the department employs certain merger guidelines regarding the acceptability of prospective mergers.

While it is difficult to draw direct parallels between the nature of competition in the securities industry and these guidelines, it is worth noting that the department uses rather rigid standards on horizontal mergers when the C4 concentration ratio is greater than 75 percent. A stricter standard is also applied in markets with at least some degree of concentration and in which "any grouping of the largest firms in the market from the two largest to the eight largest" has increased by approximately 7 percent or more over a period of five to ten years. The above statistical results give some indication of the extent to which this guideline might become relevant in the investment banking industry.

3. Functions and Strategies of Investment Banks

1. Since many of the clients of American investment banks are U.S.-based multinational companies, there is also an international dimension to the services they provide. The activities listed in the text are in large part duplicated for the foreign markets, thereby doubling the differentiating characteristics of firms. Here we will confine ourselves to the U.S. market; we briefly consider the competitive implications of foreign markets in the concluding chapter.

2. See, for instance, various issues of the SIA's periodical, *Trends*. Since our data were compiled, the SIA has revised its nomenclature to conform with that of the SEC. "National Wirehouses" are now called "National Full Line" firms.

3. Since the cut-off date of the study, mergers have reduced the number by two. Blyth Eastman has been absorbed into Paine Webber, and Loeb Rhoades has combined with Shearson.

4. Wyndham Robinson, "The Underwriters Have to Offer Even More," *Fortune*, Jan. 1973, p. 116.

5. The barriers to acquiring an institutional brokerage-distribution capability do not appear to be high. See for instance, Samuel L. Hayes III, "The Transformation of Investment Banking," *Harvard Business Review*, Jan.–Feb. 1979, p. 155.

6. Irwin Friend and Marshall E. Blume, "Competitive Commissions on the New York Stock Exchange," *Journal of Finance*, Sept. 1973, pp. 795–819.

7. See, for instance, *Wall Street Letter*, March 10, 1980, p. 4; also see Paine Webber News Release, Dec. 21, 1979, p. 2.

4. The Major Investment Banks and Their Client Bases

1. *Institutional Investor* ceased publishing this annual feature after 1979, and explained to us that this was done because of the increasing difficulty in identifying appropriate client affiliations. It should also be noted that the magazine revised somewhat its criteria for affiliation during the years covered in this study.

2. We surveyed all of the top 20 firms in our sample to determine the extent to which the firms themselves perceived that there were errors in the *Institutional Investor* list. In telephone interviews with a corporate finance partner at each firm, we compiled a "Who's With Whom" list as seen by each firm involved (using similar criteria to those employed by *Institutional Investor*). The results showed that there was disagreement in 10–15 percent of the cases as to the client-bank relationships.

3. Of course, sheer numbers of clients mask size, frequency of issue, and other criteria that could significantly alter the real market power enjoyed by certain investment banks.

4. The reverse is a more controversial proposition; stability of bank-client relationships need not signal strongly that competition is weak.

5. The Matching of Banks and Clients

1. For those with a quantitative bent, a certain amount of comment about notation will facilitate the discussion. Suppose that investment banks are numbered $i = 1, \ldots, I$. Clients similarly are numbered $j = 1, \ldots, J$. Let x_i be a vector of attributes of bank i. Let y_j be a vector of attributes of client j. Let $B = x_1, \ldots, x_I$ be the set of banks from which clients can choose. Let $P(x_i, y_j \mid B)$ be the probability that a client with characteristics y_j would choose a bank with characteristics x_i, given a field of choice of B. The logit model takes the form

$$P(x_i, y_j \mid B) = \frac{E(u(x_i, y_j))}{\sum_{e \in B} E(u(x_e, y_j))}$$

where $E(u) = e^{\lambda u}$.

The function $u(x_i, y_j)$ measure of the value of bank with attributes x_i to a client with attributes y_j. In the logit model, the function u has a particular form:

$$u(x_i, y_j) = \sum_k \beta_k v_k (x_i, y_j)$$

where the $v_k(x, y)$ are known numerical functions and the β_k are parameters to be estimated. The problem is to specify the functions $v_k(x, y)$ to embody our hypotheses about the causes of choice and matching in this market and then to estimate the weights, using data on the actual matchings of clients and banks in the market. For a review of the logit model see D. McFadden, "Conditional Logit Analysis of Qualitative Choice Behavior," in P. Zarembka, ed., *Frontiers of Econometrics* (New

York: Academic Press, 1973).

2. The logit model has a property known as the independence of irrelevant alternatives, which is generally thought to be empirically desirable. With the size of the choice set, the number of choosers, and the length of the variable list, it is not computationally feasible to test more general choice models, ones that do not impose this property. There are statistical tests of the assumption of independence of irrelevant alternatives. Strictly they are joint tests of the logit specification and the particular variables employed. See D. A. Hausman and D. McFadden. "Specification Tests for the Multinominal Logit Model," M.I.T. Department of Economics Working Paper no. 292, Oct. 1981. The model here does not pass the tests, and hence it should be regarded as merely the best currently practicable approximation to reality.

3. It should be noted that for banks with a dummy variable, the market share is predicted perfectly for the usual regression-type reasons.

6. Competitive Groups in the Industry

1. Two of the 20 banks, Lazard Frères and Shearson, drop out for lack of data.

2. Banks could be linked to each other in a chain-like fashion so that any attempt to group them by a procedure such as this one would fail. What is striking and interesting is that they can in fact be grouped cleanly in this way.

3. If we treat each group as a bank, construct the group probabilities of attracting each client, g_{ij}, for group i and corporation j, and construct the correlation coefficients between pairs of vectors $G_i = (g_{i1}, g_{i2}, \ldots, g_{ij})$, we get the numbers in table 27. The same data are presented schematically in figure 15.

Index